THE *Best* OF SMITH WIGGLESWORTH

ACCESS THE

MIRACULOUS

IF YOU WOULD

ONLY
BELIEVE

THE *Best* OF
SMITH
WIGGLESWORTH

WHITAKER
HOUSE

All Scripture quotations are taken from the *New King James Version*, © 1979, 1980, 1982 by Thomas Nelson, Inc. Used by permission. All rights reserved. Scripture quotations marked (KJV) are taken from the King James Version of the Holy Bible.

This new edition from Whitaker House has been updated for the modern reader. Words, expressions, and sentence structure have been revised for clarity and readability. Although the NKJV translation quoted in this edition was not available to the author, the Bible versions used were prayerfully selected in order to make the language of the entire text readily understandable while maintaining the author's original premises and message.

**THE BEST OF SMITH WIGGLESWORTH:
Access the Miraculous If You Would Only Believe**

This anthology includes excerpts from:

Smith Wigglesworth on Faith
ISBN: 978-0-88368-531-0
© 1998 by Whitaker House

Smith Wigglesworth on God's Power
ISBN: 978-1-64123-124-4
© 2000 by Whitaker House

Smith Wigglesworth on the Holy Spirit
ISBN: 978-0-88368-544-0
© 1999 by Whitaker House

Smith Wigglesworth on Healing
ISBN: 978-0-88368-426-9
© 1999 by Whitaker House

Smith Wigglesworth on Spirit-Filled Living
ISBN: 978-0-88368-534-1
© 1998 by Whitaker House

Wigglesworth on the Anointing
ISBN: 978-0-88368-530-3
© 2000 by Whitaker House

Smith Wigglesworth on Spiritual Gifts
ISBN: 978-0-88368-533-4
© 1998 by Whitaker House

Smith Wigglesworth Only Believe
ISBN: 978-0-88368-996-7
© 1998 by Whitaker House

Ever Increasing Faith
ISBN: 978-0-88368-633-1
© 2001 by Whitaker House

Smith Wigglesworth on Heaven
ISBN: 978-0-88368-954-7
© 1998 by Whitaker House

ISBN: 978-1-64123-323-1
eBook ISBN: 978-1-64123-324-8
Printed in the United States of America
© 2019 by Whitaker House

Whitaker House
1030 Hunt Valley Circle
New Kensington, PA 15068
www.whitakerhouse.com

Library of Congress Cataloging-in-Publication Data (Pending)

1 2 3 4 5 6 7 8 9 10 11 ⨆⨆ 26 25 24 23 22 21 20 19

Contents

Smith Wigglesworth on Faith

1

Only Believe

I want you to be full of joy, enough joy to fill a deep well. If you have to make it happen, there is something wrong. If God makes it happen, there is always something right. We must be careful to see that God means something greater for us than we have ever touched.

GO FORWARD

I have thought a great deal about momentum. I find there is such a thing as trusting in the past. When a train has gotten to a certain place, some people get out, but some go on to the end of the journey. Let us go far enough. There is only one thing to do: stay fully aware and always be pressing on. It will not do to trust in the past. Let us go forward. When it comes to the power of momentum, the past will not do. We must have an inflow of the life of God manifested, because we are in that place of manifestation.

I want you to sing now what I sing in all my meetings: "Only Believe."

> Only believe, only believe,
> > All things are possible, only believe.
> Only believe, only believe,
> > All things are possible, only believe.

The importance of that chorus is that right there in the middle of it is that word *only*. If I can get you to see that when you can get rid of yourself and your human help and everything else and have only God behind you, then you have reached a place of great reinforcement. You have reached a place of continual success. If you help yourself—in the measure you help yourself—you will find that the life of God and the power of God are diminished.

I find so many people trying to help themselves. What God wants is for us to cling to Him absolutely and entirely. There is only one grand plan that God has for us: *"Only believe"* (Mark 5:36). If we believe, we will have absolute rest and perfect submission. When God has entirely taken charge of the situation, you are absolutely brought into everything that God has, because you dare to *"only believe"* what He says.

Conditions on God's side are always beyond your asking or thinking. The conditions on your side cannot reach the other side unless you come into a place where you can rest on the omnipotent plan of God; then His plan cannot fail to be successful. God wants me to press into your heart a living truth: only believe and have absolute rest and perfect tranquility and allow God to absolutely take charge of the whole situation. You can then say, "God has said it, and it cannot fail." All His promises are *"Yes"* and *"Amen"* to those who believe. (See

2 Corinthians 1:20.) Are you ready to sing it now? Only believe. Only believe. All things are possible; only believe.

THREE IS NO CONDEMNATION

Look at Romans 8:1–17. We have a tremendously big subject before us, but it will be one that will be helpful. It is in the realm of spiritual vitality. I want to speak to you on life because I find that there is nothing that is going to help you reach, press in to, or live this higher life, except this divine life, which will always help us if we yield ourselves absolutely to it. We not only get exercised by this divine light, but we are kept in perfect rest, because God is giving us rest. And it is needed in this day, for this is a day when people everywhere are becoming self-contented in natural things, and when everywhere there is no definite cry or prayer within the soul that is making people cease from everything and cry out for God and the coming of the Son.

So I am intensely eager and full of desire that I may by some means quicken or move you on to a place where you will see what the Spirit has for you. Life in Christ is absolutely different from death. Life is what people long for because of everything it has in it. Death is what people draw back from because of what it has in it. This light of the life of the Spirit, which God wants me to bring before you, is where God has designed for us to live, in freedom from the law of sin and death.

So you can see I have a great subject, which is from the divine mind of the Master. You remember what the Master said. He said that He who lives for himself will die. He who seeks to live will die, but he who is willing to die will live. (See Luke 17:33.) God wants us to see that there is a life that is contrary to this life.

The Spirit of the Lord reveals the following to us in the Word of God: *"He who believes in the Son has everlasting life; and he who does not believe the Son shall not see life"* (John 3:36). The unbelieving person is living and walking about but not seeing life. There is a life that is always brought into condemnation, which is living in death. There is a life that is free from condemnation—living in the Life.

AN INTERPRETATION OF TONGUES

God the Author, the Finisher, the bringing into, the expression in the human life, changing it from that downward grade and lifting it and bringing it into a place of revelation to see that God has designed me to be greater than anything in the world.

I want you all to understand today that the design of God's Son for us is to be so much greater in this world than we have ever comprehended. God's design is not for me to stay where I was when I came into this room. God's plan is that the spiritual revelation will bring me into touch with a divine harmony. God wants me to touch ideals today; He wants me to reach something more. My eyes are looking up; my heart is looking up. My heart is big and enlarged in the presence of God, for I want to hear one word from God: "Come up higher." God will give us that—the privilege of going higher into a holy association.

There is a word of helpfulness in the first verse of Romans 8: *"There is therefore now no condemnation."* This is the most important thing in all the world; there is nothing to be compared to it. It is beyond all you can think. The person who is under no condemnation has the heavens opened above him. This person has the smile of God upon him. This person has come into the realm of faith and joy and knows that his prayers are answered. I know that He hears me when I pray—I know I have the petition.

So God the Holy Spirit would have us to understand that there is a place in the Holy Spirit where there is no condemnation. This place is holiness, purity, righteousness, higher ground, perfection, and being more perfected in the presence of God. This higher ground state is holy desire. It is perfection where God is bringing us to live in such a way that He may smile through us and act upon us until our bodies become a flame of light ignited by Omnipotence. This is God's plan for us in the inheritance. It is an inheritance in the race that God wants us in today. This race, this divine race, this crowned race, this divine place is for us today.

There is no condemnation. The great secret of the plan of God for those who are in it is to see our covering. Oh, the covering; oh, the enfolding; oh, those eyes, those lovely eyes, that lovely Jesus, that blessed assurance of being strengthened, that knowledge of the Rock of Ages cleft for me, that place where I know I am! And that joy unbounding where I know there are neither devils nor angels nor principalities nor powers to interfere with that life in Christ! (See Romans 8:38–39.) It is wonderful!

"No weapon formed against you shall prosper" (Isaiah 54:17). God makes us devil-proof, whether evil reports or good reports (see 2 Corinthians 6:8) are spread about us. The power of the Most High God has put us in Christ. If we had put ourselves in, it would have been different. We were in the world, but God took us out of the world and put us into Christ, so God today by His Spirit wants us to see how this regenerative power, this glorious principle of God's high thoughtfulness, is for us. God wants me to leave myself in His sweetness. Oh, there is a sweetness about the Lord; oh, there is a

glorious power behind us when God is behind us; there is a wonderful going before when He goes before us. He said, "I will go before you, and I will be your rear guard." (See Isaiah 52:12.) And so I see that God the Holy Spirit wants me today to penetrate or bring forth or show forth the glorious joy there is in this wonderful incarnation of the Spirit for us all in Christ Jesus. Glory to God!

> It reaches me, it reaches me,
> Wondrous grace it reaches me,
> Pure, exhaustless, ever flowing,
> Wondrous grace it reaches me.

THE WORD MAKES US FREE

I can see this order of life that God has for us now: it is to make me free from the law of sin and the law of death. Praise the Lord! And I find that all sin leads down; it is like gravity. But I find that all faith lifts up into a place of admiration of God. So God wants to spread forth His wings and show that He is able, He is Almightiness, and He is able to preserve what we have committed to Him, because He is our Lord. He is not only our Creator, but also the One who preserves us. He has not only redeemed me, but He is also preserving me. I see I cannot do any of these things by myself, but He has made it possible that if I believe, He will do it.

I absolutely believe that the Word I am preaching to you is sent forth by the power of the Spirit. I find that God has strengthened your hands and is preparing you for the race, the race that is set before you. (See Hebrews 12:1.) It is the divine plan I want to ask for in my life so that I may be absolutely in the place where I am preserved from all evil. These are days when Satan seeks to be very great. Oh, yes, he is tremendously busy seeking those whom he may devour (see 1 Peter 5:8), but I am finding out that God has blessed me and has blessed us so that we will be in a place where we are more than overcomers (see Romans 8:37).

Being more than overcomers is to have a shout at the end of the fight. It not only means overcoming, but it also means being able to stand when we have overcome, and not fall down. I count it a great privilege that God has opened my eyes to see that His great plan has been arranged for us before the foundation of the world, and we may all just come into line with God to believe that these things that He has promised must come to pass to whoever believes.

Turn back once more to the thought that no man, whoever he is, will ever make progress unless he learns that he is greater than the Adversary. If you don't learn, if you don't understand, if you don't come into line today with the thought that you are greater than the Adversary, you will find out that you have a struggle in your life. I want to breathe through you today a passage that is in Scripture, which is, *"He who is in you"* (1 John 4:4). I don't want to take anybody out of his bearings; I want to be so simple that everyone who hears this truth will know that he has a fortification, that he has the oracles of God behind him. In truth he has the power of God with him to overcome Satan through the blood of the Lamb. *"Who is he who overcomes…but he who believes that Jesus is the [Christ]?"* (1 John 5:5), for it is he who overcomes the world, even through his faith (see verse 4).

Now faith is the supreme, divine position where God is entrenched, not only in the life, but also through the life, the mind, and the body. You will never find that you are at all equal against the power of the Enemy except on the authority that you have an authority laid down within you. He who believes in his heart is able to move the mountain (see Mark 11:23), but you do not believe in your heart until your heart is made perfect in the presence of God. As you think in your heart, so you are. *"Blessed are the pure in heart, for they shall see God"* (Matthew 5:8). These are the people who see this truth that I am presenting to you today, and it is in them, and that makes them *"more than conquerors"* (Romans 8:37). They have life over sin, life over death, life over diseases, life over the devil. Praise the Lord!

AN INTERPRETATION OF TONGUES

God is not the Author of confusion but the Author of peace and brings to life and focuses the eye until it sees God only, and when you come there you will stand.

Oh, the thought, the standing, the pure hands, the clean hearts—God the Holy Spirit has designed this for us within the plan of this realm of grace. God's plan is hidden, lost, completely lost to the devil, who is not able to come near. God covers; He hides; we are sealed; bless the Lord! We are sealed until the day of redemption. We so believe in the authority of the Almighty that we triumph in this glorious realm. Oh, this divine touch of God to the human soul brings us all to say all things are possible.

> Praise the Lord 'tis so, praise the Lord 'tis so,
> Once I was blind but now I see,
> Once I was bound but now I am free,
> Through faith I have the victory,
> Praise the Lord 'tis so.

And so the Lord has a great plan for us today to see, or rather to bring us to our wealth in Christ. Our wealth is so rich, beyond all comparison. *"Deep calls unto deep"* (Psalm 42:7). The Lord has prepared for us not only a sonship, but also an heirship, not only an heirship, but also a joint-heirship. We are not only feeling the breath of God, but the breath of God is also moving us. We are not only touching fire, but fire is also burning everything that cannot stand fire. And so in this holy sea of life, this divine inheritance for us, I see the truth so full of joy unspeakable today, and I see it and I read it to you. *"There is therefore now no condemnation to those who are in Christ Jesus"* (Romans 8:1). Oh, hallelujah!

THE LAW OF LIFE

Then I notice clearly that we must see and we must always get the facts of these truths. It is a law. Well, there is a law of gravity, and there is a law of life, and we must see the difference and live in life that ceases to die. On the other hand, we must live a life that continues to die and to die daily, because when we die, we receive life. In that life, the baptism of the Holy Spirit is a baptism into a death, into a likeness unto death, into the Son of Man in His likeness. The baptism of the Holy Spirit is purifying, energizing, and it brings the soul to where it touches ideal immensity. God wants us to have no other plan in our mind but this.

Now come along with me, for the Lord has many things to say to us. I see that the devil wants to destroy. Now listen, you will find that John 10:10 is more real than ever. It says that the devil comes to steal because he is a thief, and then if he can steal, he will destroy: he will kill, and then he will destroy. I also find that Jesus comes along with a flood tide of refreshment and says, "I have come with life, with life and abundance of life." Abundance of life means that you live in an activity of divine inspiration, that you never touch the other thing. You are above it. You are only in association with it to pray it through or to cause the salt to be saltier or the light to be brighter until others can see the way. It is a foundation of God's principle, and everyone who knows it says that is God.

I will go a little further to help you. I find out that whatever you learn from me—I say it without fear of any contradiction—God has given you another chance of seeing light and life. If you fail to seize the opportunity, you will find you will be worse tomorrow. God speaks through me to tens of thousands all over. God is sending me forth to stir the people to diligence. Mine is not an ordinary message. You will never find I have an ordinary message. The past tense is an ordinary message. I must be on fire. The day is too late for me to stop; I must be catching fire; I must be in the wing. I am intensely in earnest and mean all I say now.

Within are the thoughts to impregnate you today with a desire from heaven, to let you see that you do not have to give place to the devil, neither in thought nor in word. And I pray to God the Holy Spirit that you will be so stirred that you will have a conviction come over your soul that you dare not disbelieve any of the truth, but rather the whole body will be aflame with the epistle of truth. *"He who has seen Me has seen the Father"* (John 14:9). Is that so? Oh, He said, "I and my Father will come and dwell in you." (See verse 23.) Yes, and when He comes to dwell in us, it is to be the epistle, it is to be the manifestation, the power; it is to be the Son of God working miracles, destroying the power of the devils, casting out evil spirits, and laying hands on the people so they who were dying under the power of the devil will live.

This is life divine, and this is God's thought for you now, if you will not fail to recognize the good hand of God coming to us, God speaking to us of these deep things of Himself that mean so much for us. Oh, bless God that I am entrusted with such a Gospel, with such a message, but first it burns in me.

You cannot bring anything to anybody else before you have reached it first yourself. You cannot talk beyond your wisdom. God brings you to test these things; then, because you desire to handle and because you chance to eat these things, out of the eating and digesting of these things will come the refining fire and the flood tide upon the dry ground. This is so because we will be a flame of fire for God: divine inspiration, catching the vision all the time and walking in the Holy Spirit. Oh, bless the Lord!

> I know the Lord, I know the Lord,
> I know the Lord has laid His hands on me.

Glory to Jesus! Is that good hand of God on me only? No! No! No! God has come to more than me, but the important thing is that we recognize the hand of God and the voice of God and that we recognize the power of God. We need to recognize how to be careful and gentle and how to have wisdom to abide in the anointing and to keep in the place where God is not only consuming fire, but also purifying fire. Glory to God! Oh, for this holy, intense zeal. Oh, that God would give us today this zealous position, which will absolutely put us in a place where we know this day that God has spoken to us. We know that once more this day God has brought before us another opportunity. This day—thank God that in His grace and kindness He has opened the way, beloved. The Lord speaks once, even more so, twice. God unfolds the kingdom to you, but He expects you to jump in and go through.

SWEPT UP IN FAITH

"There is therefore now no condemnation" (Romans 8:1). I would not trade this truth for the money in a million banks. What does it mean? There is condemnation that comes to us if we know that we ought to be further on in the race than we are. Something has stopped us.

Freedom from condemnation means so much to me. I know I was baptized with the Holy Spirit. The Holy Spirit was not the life; Jesus is the life, but the Holy Spirit came to reveal the life. The Holy Spirit is not truth; Jesus is the truth, but the Holy Spirit is the Spirit of that truth. So I must see that God has so much for me today. I notice that to be without condemnation I must be in the just place with God.

It is a wonderful thing to be justified by faith, but I find there is a greater place of justification than this. I find this: because Abraham believed God, He accounted it to him as righteousness. (See Romans 4:3.) That was more than the other. God accounted it to him as righteousness because Abraham believed God. He imputed no sin, and therefore He gave him wings. When He imputed no sin, He lifted Abraham into the righteousness of God, lifted him out of himself into a place of rest, and God covered him there. Abraham has not received anything from the Lord that He is not willing to give to anyone now. I am seeing today that whatever I have reached, I am only on the rippling of the wave of the surface of God's intense zeal of love and compassion. He is always saying nothing less than this: "Come on." So I am going forward.

I am here with a whole heart to say, "Come with me," for the Lord has spoken good concerning His people, and He will give them the land of promise. *"No good thing will He withhold"* (Psalm 84:11). So I know that God is in the place to bless today, but I want you to catch the fire. I want you to come out of all your natural propensities, for I tell you nothing is as detrimental to your spiritual rising as your natural mind and your body. Nothing will destroy your spiritual life but your own self. Paul knew that, and therefore he said, "I count myself as rubbish." (See Philippians 3:8.)

Is there anything else? Yes! Paul said, *"I did not immediately confer with flesh and blood"* (Galatians 1:16). He was getting very near this truth. I tell you there are a good many natural associations. As a Jew he came over to the plan of redemption, where everything was absolute foolishness and rank hypocrisy in Jewish estimation.

Is there anything else? Certainly! "If I can only win Him." (See Philippians 3:8.) Oh, what understanding there was in Paul, what beautiful character! What God had revealed to him about this Nazarene King was worthy to make him come into line to see. I can understand today that God breathed upon Paul absolutely. It is the breath of divine order; it is the breath of desire. God breathes on, and as He breathed on him I see this.

Oh, to know! To know that so many years ago, God baptized me, and I can say without a shadow of a doubt that God has swept me on. You know it! How I have always longed to go. I tell you, if you come there, you will have to say "no" to a thousand things in your natural order, for your own hearts will deceive you. Be careful of your friends and relatives; they are always a damp rag or a wet blanket. God wants us to lean on Him and go on with Him and dare to believe Him. There is no condemnation. (See Romans 8:1.)

Oh, how sweet the thought! Never mind, I am not here to crush or to bruise anyone. I am here in the Holy Spirit order I know: to make you long to come on, long to obey, long to say to everything that is not the high order of holiness, "Regardless of who misses the right path, I will go through."

> I'm going through, Jesus, I'm going through,
>> I'll pay the price whatever others do,
> I'll take the way of the Lord's despised few,
>> I'm going through, Jesus, I'm going through.

It is worth it all, praise the Lord, worth it all. Thank God, quickened by the Spirit, I have covered over forty-four thousand miles. You cannot comprehend it with your mind; it is too vast. At all places God in His Spirit has been moving me. I have seen the glory of God moving. I have had the pleasure of seeing two thousand people in the morning and over five thousand in the evening to hear me preach. What opportunities! What times of refreshment! What wonderful things one sees, and I realize that nothing from the past would do. You cannot rely upon anything in the past, and so I am realizing the truth now. It is this: I see it is a whole burnt offering; I see it is an offering in righteousness; I see it is an offering that is accepted; and I see it is a daily offering.

No past sanctification is good enough for today, and I find that this life leads you on to see that it is sanctification with an inward desire of being more perfected every day. While I know I was wonderfully saved, I find that it is being saved that moves me toward perfection. While I see salvation has designs within it for the coming of the King, I see it enriches me with a ceaseless warmth so that

I cannot get out of it. Nothing will do unless I am absolutely heated up with this life, because I must see the King.

Since it came, Pentecost has been spoken against, and if there is not someone rising up against you, if there is not a war on, you are doing a bad job. I tell you this in sincerity, if you are not making the people mad or glad, there is something amiss with your ministry. If you leave people as you found them, God is not speaking through you. So, there must be an intensity of enlargement of this divine personality, of God in the soul, so absolutely bringing you to a place where you know it would be awful to remain two days in the same place. I do not know how it sounds, but I tell you, it is intense zeal.

Come on a little nearer now. There are opportunities. God has the right-of-way to the heart and life to bring them to a place where opportunities are made for the possibility of being accomplished. I am realizing that God must impress upon your heart around you, wherever you are, that He has an opportunity for you today. It will stand right in front of you, and by that means you will be brought into a place where you will convince the people because God is there. Without the shadow of a doubt, the Word of God is effective and destroying, and it brings about perfect life.

CLOTHED IN FAITH

I am going to close with one Scripture passage, because of the importance of it. I want to give you one more word of life. Turn with me to the fifth chapter of 2 Corinthians—it will have something to do with this important treasure. I see that if I preach anything less than these things, I find I miss the whole opportunity of my life. I must have a ministry of faith; I must have clothing for this ministry of faith; I must have the Spirit of Life to manifest this ministry of faith; and then I must have the convincing evidence through the power of the Spirit of imparting that to the lives of the people. I pray that you will lay hold of this truth.

We have here in this fifth chapter one of the best things that God has given me now for some time, this ministry of life. "For we who are in this tent groan, being burdened, not because we want to be unclothed, but further clothed, that mortality may be swallowed up by life" (verse 4). Here is one of the greatest truths that was in this Pentecostal evidence, or life in evidence, or the evidence in the life. I find that Jesus is not coming to fetch the body—that is perfectly in order, we cannot get away from the fact—but Jesus is coming for the life in the body. The body may die, but that body will not be in the glory. God will give us a body, and the only thing He is going to give is life. The life is not your life, but it is His life in you. He who dwells in God has God dwelling in him. (See 1 John 4:16). Jesus came to give us His life. Paul says, "Now I live, yet not I, but He lives His life." (See Galatians 2:20.) In Colossians we read that when He who is our life appears, then we will appear. (See Colossians 3:4).

You will find that you do not have a desire outside the desire of pleasing Him. There is a joy, or fullness of expression of all the joy, where you see His life being manifested in your mortal body, and that makes you so free from the natural life. Then you are joined up to the supernatural. Paul said he wanted to go, not to be unclothed but clothed upon. (See 2 Corinthians 5:4). There is a thought. Do we want to go? No! No! That is not the order of the body; that is not the order of the natural man; that is not the order of the human. What does he want? He wants to be so clothed upon; that is the first thing, clothed upon. When? Now!

Is there anything else? Yes! It is the life clothed upon and the life within the body eating up every mortality, every sense, every human desire, everything that has caused grief, sorrow, brokenness of heart, and has interfered with our rest, stopping the shining of our faces, making us feel how sorry we are. God wants to have His way with us, live in us to eat up everything, until the body will only be a body filled with the Spirit life. Then the body will only be an existence as the temple for the Spirit. But the body will be preserved blameless. The body, the soul, the spirit in the world will be blameless, and the coming of the King will take the life and change it to present it with Him. God will bring us there.

As sure as I have had this fellowship with you in the Spirit, as sure as your heart has been warmed, I say to you: never mind the past. You may have a thousand things that spoil you; forget them. Know that God has overcome for you so that you will overcome and will be presented faultless, even more so, spotless in the presence of the King. This life will eat up mortality—hallelujah!

The law of the life of the Spirit of Christ will make you free from the law of sin and death. (See Romans 8:2.) Can I attain this today? This is a problem; "I have failed a thousand times," you say. Never mind. Is your heart warmed? Do you want to be conquered, or do you love to come into line with Him? Will you pay the price for it? What is the desire of your heart? You may be sorry for the past, but let God have you for the future. You would not like to remain as you were before you came here. I know you would not; you exactly feel the position. You say, "Lord, forgive everything of the past, but help me, Lord, today to offer an offering in righteousness before you. Today I give myself afresh."

2

By Faith

We read in the Word that by faith Abel offered unto God a more excellent sacrifice than Cain. (See Hebrews 11:4.) We also read that by faith Enoch was taken away so that he would not see death (see verse 5); by faith Noah prepared an ark to the saving of his household (see verse 7); by faith Abraham, when he was called to go out into the place that he would receive for an inheritance, obeyed (see verse 8).

There is only one way to all the treasures of God, and that is the way of faith. All things are possible, even the fulfilling of all promises is possible, to him who believes. (See Mark 9:23.) And it is all by grace; *"by grace you have been saved through faith, and that not of yourselves; it is the gift of God"* (Ephesians 2:8).

There will be failure in our lives if we do not build on the base, the Rock Christ Jesus. He is the only way. He is the truth. He is the life. And the Word He gives us is life-giving. As we receive the Word of Life, it quickens, it opens, it fills us, it moves us, it changes us, and it brings us into a place where we dare to say amen to all that God has said. Beloved, there is a lot in an amen. You never get any place until you have the amen inside of you. That was the difference between Zacharias and Mary. When the Word came to Zacharias, he was filled with unbelief until the angel said, *"You will be mute… because you did not believe my words"* (Luke 1:20). Mary said, *"Let it be to me according to your word"* (verse 38). And the Lord was pleased that she believed that there would be a performance of what He had spoken. When we believe what God has said, there will be a performance.

BELIEF BECOMES FACT

Let's look at the twelfth chapter of Acts, and we will find that there were people waiting all night and praying that Peter might come out of prison. But there seemed to be one thing missing despite all their praying, and that was faith. Rhoda had more faith than all the rest of them. When the knock came at the door, she ran to it, for she was expecting an answer to her prayers. The moment she heard Peter's voice, she ran back and announced to them that Peter was standing at the door. And all the people said, "You are mad. It isn't so." That was not faith. When she insisted that he was there, they said, "Well, perhaps God has sent his angel." (See verses 14–15.) But Rhoda insisted, "It is Peter." And Peter continued knocking. They went out and found it so. (See verse 16.) What Rhoda had believed had become a glorious fact.

Beloved, we may do much praying and groaning, but we do not receive from God because of that; we receive because we believe.

And yet sometimes it takes God a long time to bring us through the groaning and the crying before we can believe.

I know that no man by his praying can change God, for you cannot change Him. Finney said, "Can a man who is full of sin and all kinds of ruin in his life change God when he starts to pray?" No, it is impossible. But when a man labors in prayer, he groans and travails because his tremendous sin is weighing him down, and he becomes broken in the presence of God. When properly melted, he comes into perfect harmony with the divine plan of God, and then God can work in that clay. He could not before. Prayer changes hearts, but it never changes God. He is the same yesterday, and today, and forever: full of love, full of compassion, full of mercy, full of grace, and ready to bestow this and communicate that to us as we come to Him in faith.

Believe that when you come into the presence of God you can have all you came for. You can take it away, and you can use it, for all the power of God is at your disposal in response to your faith. The price for all was paid by the blood of Jesus Christ at Calvary. Oh, He is the living God, the One who has power to change us! *"It is He who has made us, and not we ourselves"* (Psalm 100:3). And it is He who purposes to transform us so that the greatness of His power may work through us. Oh, beloved, God delights in us, and when a man's ways please the Lord, then He makes all things move according to His own blessed purpose.

COMMUNION WITH GOD

We read in Hebrews 11:5, *"By faith Enoch was taken away so that he did not see death...before he was taken he had this testimony, that he pleased God."* I believe it is in the mind of God to prepare us for being taken away. But remember this, being taken away comes only on the line of holy obedience and a walk according to the good pleasure of God.

We are called to walk together with God through the Spirit. It is delightful to know that we can talk with God and hold communion with Him. Through this wonderful baptism in the Spirit that the Lord gives us, He enables us to talk to Him in a language that the Spirit has given, a language that no man understands but that He understands, a language of love. Oh, how wonderful it is to speak to Him in the Spirit, to let the Spirit lift and lift and lift us until He takes us into the very presence of God! I pray that God by His Spirit may move all of us so that we walk with God as Enoch walked with Him. But beloved, it is a walk by faith and not by sight, a walk of believing the Word of God.

I believe there are two kinds of faith. All people are born with a natural faith, but God calls us to a supernatural faith that is a gift from Himself. In the twenty-sixth chapter of Acts, Paul tells us of his call, how God spoke to him and told him to go to the Gentiles:

> To open their eyes, in order to turn them from darkness to light, and from the power of Satan to God, that they may receive forgiveness of sins and an inheritance among those who are sanctified by faith in Me.　　　　　　　　　　　(Acts 26:18)

The faith that was in Christ was to be given by the Holy Spirit to those who believed. From this point on, as Paul yielded his life to God, he could say,

> I have been crucified with Christ; it is no longer I who live, but Christ lives in me; and the life which I now live in the flesh I live by faith in the Son of God, who loved me and gave Himself for me.　　　　　　　　　　　(Galatians 2:20)

The faith of the Son of God is communicated by the Spirit to the one who puts his trust in God and in His Son.

UNDERSTAND GOD'S WORD

I believe that all our failures come because of an imperfect understanding of God's Word. I see that it is impossible to please God on any other line except by faith, and everything that is not of faith is sin. (See Romans 14:23.) You say, "How can I obtain this faith?" You see the secret in Hebrews 12:2: *"Looking unto Jesus, the author and finisher of our faith."* He is the Author of faith. Oh, the might of our Christ, who created the universe and upholds it all by the might of His power! God has chosen Him and ordained Him and clothed Him, and He who made this vast universe will make us a new creation. He spoke the Word, and the stars came into being; can He not speak the Word that will produce a mighty faith in us? This One who is the Author and Finisher of our faith comes and dwells within us, quickens us by His Spirit, and molds us by His will. He comes to live His life of faith within us and to be to us all that we need. And He who has begun a good work within us will complete it and perfect it (see Philippians 1:6), for He is not only the Author but also the Finisher and Perfecter of our faith (see Hebrews 12:2.)

> *For the word of God is living and powerful, and sharper than any two-edged sword, piercing even to the division of soul and spirit, and of joints and marrow, and is a discerner of the thoughts and intents of the heart.* (Hebrews 4:12)

How the Word of God severs the soul and the spirit—the soul that has a lot of carnality, a lot of selfishness in it, a lot of evil in it! Thank God, the Lord can sever from us all that is earthly and sensual and make us a spiritual people. He can bring all our selfishness to the place of death and bring the life of Jesus into our being to take the place of that earthly and sensual thing that is destroyed by the living Word.

The Word of God comes in to separate us from everything that is not of God. It destroys. It also gives life. He must bring to death all that is carnal in us. It was after the death of Christ that God raised Him up on high, and as we are dead with Him, we are raised up and made to sit in heavenly places in the new life that the Spirit gives.

God has come to lead us out of ourselves into Himself and to take us from the ordinary into the extraordinary, from the human into the divine, and to make us after the image of His Son. Oh, what a Savior! What an ideal Savior! It is written,

> *Beloved, now we are children of God; and it has not yet been re-vealed what we shall be, but we know that when He is revealed, we shall be like Him, for we shall see Him as He is.*
>
> (1 John 3:2)

But even now, the Lord wants to transform us from glory to glory, by the Spirit of the living God. Have faith in God, have faith in the Son, have faith in the Holy Spirit; and the triune God will work in you to will and to do all the good pleasure of His will. (See Philippians 2:13.)

3

Like Precious Faith

We are so dull of comprehension because we so often let the cares of this world blind our eyes, but if we can be open to God we will see that He has a greater plan for us in the future than we have ever seen or dreamed of in the past. It is God's delight to make possible to us what seems impossible, and when we reach a place where He alone has the right-of-way, then all the things that have been misty and misunderstood are cleared up.

GOD'S GIFT TO US

Let's look at 2 Peter 1:1–8:

To those who have obtained like precious faith with us by the righteousness of our God and Savior Jesus Christ: Grace and peace be multiplied to you in the knowledge of God and of Jesus our Lord, as His divine power has given to us all things that pertain to life and godliness, through the knowledge of Him who called us by glory and virtue, by which have been given to us exceedingly great and precious promises, that through these you may be partakers of the divine nature, having escaped the corruption that is in the world through lust. But also for this very reason, giving all diligence, add to your faith virtue, to virtue knowledge, to knowledge self-control, to self-control perseverance, to perseverance godliness, to godliness brotherly kindness, and to brotherly kindness love. For if these things are yours and abound, you will be neither barren nor unfruitful in the knowledge of our Lord Jesus Christ.

This *"like precious faith"* that Peter was writing about is a gift that God is willing to give to all of us, and I believe God wants us to receive it so that we may subdue kingdoms, work righteousness, and, if the time has come, to stop the mouths of lions. (See Hebrews 11:33.) Under all circumstances we should be able to triumph, not because we have confidence in ourselves, but because our confidence is only in God. It is always those people who are full of faith who have a good report, who never murmur, who are in the place of victory, who are not in the place of human order but of divine order, since God has come to dwell in them.

The Lord Jesus is the divine Author and brings into our minds the "Thus says the Lord" every time. We cannot have anything in our lives, except when we have a "Thus says the Lord" for it. We must see to it that the Word of God is always the standard of everything.

This *"like precious faith"* is for us all. But there may be some hindrance in your life that God will have to deal with. At one point in my life, it seemed as if I had had so much pressure come over my life to break me up like a potter's vessel. There is no other way into the deep things of God except by a broken spirit. There is no other way into the power of God. God will do for us exceedingly abundantly above all we ask or think (see Ephesians 3:20) when He can bring us to the place where we can say with Paul, "I live no longer" (see Galatians 2:20), and Another, even Christ, has taken the reins and the rule.

We are no better than our faith. Whatever your estimation is of your ability, or your righteousness, you are no better than your faith. No one is ever any better than his faith. He who believes that Jesus is the Son of God overcomes the world. (See 1 John 5:5.) How? This Jesus, upon whom your faith is placed—the power of His name, His personality, His life, His righteousness—are all made yours through faith. As you believe in Him and set your hope only on Him, you are purified even as He is pure. You are strengthened because He in whom you trust is strong. You are made whole because He who is all your confidence is whole. You may receive of His fullness, all the untold fullness of Christ, as your faith rests wholly in Him.

I understand God by His Word. I cannot understand God by impressions or feelings. I cannot get to know God by sentiments. If I am going to know God, I am going to know Him by His Word. I know I will be in heaven, but I cannot determine from my feelings that I am going to heaven. I am going to heaven because God's Word says it, and I believe God's Word. And *"faith comes by hearing, and hearing by the word of God"* (Romans 10:17).

GOD'S REAL WORKING

There is one thing that can hinder our faith: a conscience that is seared. Paul sought to have a conscience void of offense. (See Acts 24:16) There is a conscience that is seared, and there is a conscience that is so opened to the presence of God that the smallest thing in the world will drive it to God. What we need is a conscience that is so opened to God that not one thing can come into and stay in our lives to break up our fellowship with God and shatter our faith in Him. And when we can come into the presence of God with clear consciences and genuine faith, our hearts not condemning us, then we have confidence toward God (see 1 John 3:21), "*and whatever we ask we receive from Him*" (verse 22).

In Mark 11:24 we read, "*Therefore I say to you, whatever things you ask when you pray, believe that you receive them, and you will have them.*" Verse twenty-three speaks of mountains removed and difficulties cleared away. Sugarcoating won't do. We must have reality, the real working of our God. We must know God. We must be able to go in and converse with God. We must also know the mind of God toward us, so that all our petitions are always on the line of His will.

As this "*like precious faith*" becomes a part of you, it will make you so that you will dare to do anything. And remember, God wants daring men: men who will dare all, men who will be strong in Him and dare to do exploits. How will we reach this place of faith? Give up your own mind. Let go of your own thoughts, and take the thoughts of God, the Word of God. If you build yourself on imaginations, you will go wrong. You have the Word of God, and it is enough.

A man gave this remarkable testimony concerning the Word: "Never compare this Book with other books. Comparisons are dangerous. Never think or say that this Book contains the Word of God. It is the Word of God. It is supernatural in origin, eternal in duration, inexpressible in value, infinite in scope, regenerative in power, infallible in authority, universal in interest, personal in application, inspired in totality. Read it through. Write it down. Pray it in. Work it out. And then pass it on."

And truly the Word of God changes a man until he becomes an epistle of God. It transforms his mind, changes his character, moves him on from grace to grace, makes him an inheritor of the very nature of God. God comes in, dwells in, walks in, talks through, and dines with him who opens his being to the Word of God and receives the Spirit who inspired it.

When I was going over to New Zealand and Australia, there were many there to see me off. An Indian doctor rode in the same car with me to the docks and boarded the same ship. He was very quiet and took in all the things that were said on the ship. I began to preach, of course, and the Lord began to work among the people. In the second class of the ship, there was a young man and his wife who were attendants for a lady and gentleman in the first class. And as these two young people heard me talking to them privately and otherwise, they were very much impressed. Then the lady they were attending got very sick. In her sickness and her loneliness, she could find no relief. They called in the doctor, and the doctor gave her no hope.

And then, when in this strange dilemma—she was a great Christian Scientist, a preacher of it, and had gone many places preaching it—they thought of me. Knowing the conditions, and what she lived for, knowing that it was late in the day, that in the condition of her mind she could only receive the simplest word, I said to her, "Now you are very sick, and I won't talk to you about anything except this: I will pray for you in the name of Jesus, and the moment I pray you will be healed."

And the moment I prayed she was healed. That was this *"like precious faith"* in operation. Then she was disturbed. I showed her the terrible state she was in and pointed out to her all her folly and the fallacy of her position. I showed her that there was nothing in Christian Science, that it is a lie from the beginning and one of the last agencies of hell. At best it is a lie: preaching a lie and producing a lie.

Then she came to her senses. She became so penitent and brokenhearted. But the thing that stirred her first was that she had to go preach the simple gospel of Christ where she had preached Christian Science. She asked me if she had to give up certain things. I won't mention the things; they are too vile. I said, "No, what you have to do is to see Jesus and take Jesus." When she saw the Lord in His purity, the other things had to go. At the presence of Jesus, all else goes.

This opened the door. I had to preach to all on the boat. This gave me a great chance. As I preached, the power of God fell, conviction came, and sinners were saved. They followed me into my cabin one after another. God was working there.

Then this Indian doctor came. He said, "What will I do? Your preaching has changed me, but I must have a foundation. Will you spend some time with me?"

"Of course I will."

Then we went alone, and God broke the fallow ground. This Indian doctor was going right back to his Indian conditions under a new order. He had left a practice there. He told me of the great practice he had. He was going back to his practice to preach Jesus.

If you have lost your hunger for God, if you do not have a cry for more of God, you are missing the plan. A cry must come up from us that cannot be satisfied with anything but God. He wants to give us the vision of the prize ahead that is something higher than we have ever attained. If you ever stop at any point, pick up at the place where you have left off, and begin again under the refining light and power of heaven. God will meet you. And while He will bring you to a consciousness of your own frailty and to a brokenness of spirit, your faith will lay hold of Him and all the divine resources. His light and compassion will be manifested through you, and He will send the rain.

Should we not dedicate ourselves afresh to God? Some say, "I dedicated myself last night to God." Every new revelation brings a new decision. Let us seek Him.

Smith Wigglesworth on God's Power

4

We Mean Business with God

There is a power in God's Word that brings life where death is. *"Only believe"* (Mark 5:36). *"Only believe."* Jesus said that the time will come when *"the dead will hear the voice of the Son of God; and those who hear will live"* (John 5:25). For he who believes this Word, *"all things are possible to him who believes"* (Mark 9:23). The life of the Son is in the Word, and all who are saved can preach this Word. This Word frees us from death and corruption; it is life in the nature. Jesus *"brought life and immortality to light through the gospel"* (2 Timothy 1:10).

We can never exhaust the Word; it is so abundant. *"There is a river whose streams...make glad the city of God"* (Psalm 46:4); its source is in the glory. The essence of its life is God. The life of Jesus embodied is its manifested power.

INTERPRETATION OF TONGUES

Jesus Himself has come into death and has given us the victory; the victorious Son of God in humanity overcomes, He who succors the needy. Immortality produced in mortality has changed the situation for us. This is life indeed and the end of death, Christ having "brought life and immortality to life through the Gospel."

THE NEW CHURCH ESTABLISHED

We have a wonderful subject tonight because of its manifestation of the nature of the church, for in God's first church, no lie could live. The new church that the Holy Spirit is building has no lie, but purity and *"holiness to the LORD"* (Jeremiah 2:3). I see the new church established in the breath of the Lord. God is working in a supernatural way, making faces shine with His glory, creating people so in likeness with Him that they love what is right, hate iniquity and evil, and deeply reverence Him, so that a lie is unable to remain in their midst.

"There is therefore now no condemnation to those who are in Christ Jesus, who do not walk according to the flesh, but according to the Spirit" (Romans 8:1). No one can condemn you. Many may try, but God's Word says,

> *Who shall bring a charge against God's elect? It is God who justifies. Who is he who condemns? It is Christ who died, and furthermore is also risen, who is even at the right hand of God, who also makes intercession for us.* (Romans 8:33–34)

Will Jesus condemn the sheep for whom He died? He died to save men, and He saves all who believe.

God is purifying our hearts by faith. God has come forth, clothing us with His Spirit's might, living in the blaze of this glorious day—for there is nothing greater than the Gospel.

In Acts 5, we read that Ananias and Sapphira were moved to bring an offering. (See verse 1.) The day will come when we will consider nothing as our own, because we will be so taken up with the Lord. The church will ripen into coming glory. The first day was a measure; the latter day was to be more generous.

Ananias and Sapphira sold a possession; it was their own, but when it was sold, it looked like so much money. They reasoned, "The Pentecostal order is new; it might dry up." So they agreed to give a part and reserve the other. (See verse 2.) Satan is very subtle. Many people miss the greatest things by drawing aside. Let us pay our vows to the Lord. (See Psalm 116:14, 18.)

"But Peter said, 'Ananias, why has Satan filled your heart to lie to the Holy Spirit and keep back part of the price of the land for yourself?'" (Acts 5:3). The moment Ananias and Sapphira lied to the Holy Spirit by presenting only a portion of the money to the apostles, they were struck down. (See verses 2–11.)

God has shown us a new order of the Spirit in this Holy Spirit baptism. One day, when I came into my house, my wife said, "Did you come in at the front door?" I said, "No, I came in at the back." "Oh," she said. "At the front you would have seen a crowd and a man with little clothing on, crying out, 'I have committed the unpardonable sin!'"

As I went to the door, God whispered to me, "This is what I baptized you in the Spirit for." The man came in crying, "I have committed the unpardonable sin!" I said, "You lying devil, come out, in Jesus' name." The man said, "What is it? I am free. Thank God, I never committed the unpardonable sin." The moment the lying spirit was gone, he was able to speak the truth. I realized then the power in the baptism of the Holy Spirit. It was the Spirit who said, "This is what I baptized you for," and I believe we ought to be in the place where we will always be able to understand the mind of the Spirit amid all the other voices in the world.

PURITY OF LIFE BEFORE GOD

When Ananias and Sapphira died, great fear came upon the church. (See Acts 5:5, 11.) It demonstrated the believers' love for God in that they feared to grieve Him. Why, they could ask and receive anything from God.

The church is to be of one accord, with perfect faithfulness, love, oneness, and consolation. God can lift the church into a place of manifested reconciliation and oneness, until the devil has no power in our midst, and God is smiling on us all the time.

"And through the hands of the apostles many signs and wonders were done among the people" (verse 12). A purity of life before God means a manifested power among men, with multitudes gathered into the kingdom of God. God has mightily blessed the work at Elim Tabernacle, where this meeting is taking place. Those of you who are still lingering outside the kingdom, yield to God. Get *"clean hands"* and a right purpose (see Psalm 24:4), join what is holy and on fire, and mean business for God.

"And believers were increasingly added to the Lord, multitudes of both men and women" (Acts 5:14). Oh, for this kind of revival, God breaking forth everywhere and London swept by the power of God!

There must be a great moving among us, a oneness of heart and soul, and revival is sure to come as God moves upon the people.

> *They brought the sick out into the streets and laid them on beds and couches, that at least the shadow of Peter passing by might fall on some of them. Also a multitude gathered from the surrounding cities to Jerusalem, bringing sick people and those who were tormented by unclean spirits, and they were all healed.*
>
> (Acts 5:15–16)

Unity has the effect of manifesting the work of God every time. Glory to God, it is so lovely. The people had such a living faith; they were of one heart, one mind. They thought, "Oh, if only Peter's shadow passes over our sick ones, God will heal them."

Have faith. God will heal the land. Oneness of heart and mind on the part of the church means signs and wonders in all lands. *"Whatever things you ask when you pray, believe that you receive them, and you will have them"* (Mark 11:24). *"Only believe"* (Mark 5:36). I see, beloved, that we need to get more love, and the Lord will do it. How the Master can move among the needy and perishing when He has the right of way in the church!

The finest thing is persecution. We must have a ministry that makes the people glad and the devil mad. Never mind if the people run away, for conviction is within, and God has them. And if the people are glad, the Lord also has them, so it works both ways. Don't be disturbed at anything. Remember that it was written of the Master, *"Zeal for Your house has eaten Me up"* (John 2:17). We need to have a melting, moving, broken condition—*"as poor, yet making many rich; as having nothing, and yet possessing all things"* (2 Corinthians 6:10). Let us be in harmony with the divine plan, having knowledge cemented with love, death to the old nature having perfect place in us, so that the lifepower can be manifested.

I once went for weekend meetings, and when I arrived on Saturday night, it was snowing hard, and the man meeting me stood at the door of the hall laden with packages. As we walked home, when we reached the first lamppost, I said, "Brother, are you baptized in the Holy Spirit?" Then I said, "Say you will be tonight." As we went along, at every lamppost (nearly a hundred), I repeated the question, "Say you will be baptized tonight." So he began wishing I was not staying at his house. At last we reached the gate to his house. I jumped over it and said, "Now, don't you come in here unless you say you will be baptized with the Holy Spirit tonight." "Oh," he said, "I feel so funny, but I will say it." We went in. I asked his wife, "Are you baptized in the Holy Spirit?" She said, "Oh, I want to be—but supper is ready, come in." I said, "No supper until you are both baptized in the Holy Spirit."

Did God answer? Oh yes, soon they were both speaking in tongues. Now, I believe that God will baptize you. Put up your hands and ask Him to. Also, those seeking healing and salvation, do the same, and God will meet you, every one. Amen.

5

After You Have Received Power

In Acts 1:8, we read, *"You shall receive power when the Holy Spirit has come upon you."* Oh, the power of the Holy Spirit—the power that quickens, reveals, and prevails! I love the thought that Jesus wanted all His people to have power, that He wanted all men to be overcomers. Nothing but this power of the Holy Spirit will do it—power over sin, power over sickness, power over the devil, power over all the powers of the devil! (See Luke 10:19.)

In order to understand what it means to have power, two things are necessary: one is to have *"ears to hear"* (Matthew 11:15), and the other is to have hearts to receive. Every bornagain saint of God who is filled with the Spirit has a real revelation of this truth: *"He who is in you is greater than he who is in the world"* (1 John 4:4). I say this with as much audacity as I please: I know evil spirits are in abundance and in multitudes; Jesus cast them out as legion. (See Mark 5:2–15; Luke 8:26–35.) The believer, because of the Spirit who is

51

in him, has the power to cast out the evil spirit. It *must* be so; God wants us to have this power in us; we must be able to destroy Satan's power wherever we go.

ALWAYS READY

After the Holy Spirit comes upon you, you have power. I believe a great mistake is made in these days by people waiting and waiting after they have received. After you have received, it is, "Go" (Mark 16:15). It is not, "Sit still," but *"Go into all the world and preach the gospel"* (verse 15). We will make serious havoc of the whole thing if we turn back again and crawl into a corner seeking something we already have. I want you to see that God depends on us in these last days. There is no room for anyone to boast, and the person who goes around saying, "Look at me, for I am somebody," is of no value whatever. God will not often work through such a person. He will have a people who glorify Him. He is doing what He can with what He has, but we are so unwilling to move in the plan of God that He has to grind us many times to get us where He can use us.

Jesus was so filled with the Holy Spirit that He stood in the place where He was always ready. He was always in the attitude where He brought victory out of every opportunity. The power of the Holy Spirit is within us, but it can be manifested only as we go in obedience to the opportunity before us. I believe if you wait until you think you have power after you have received the Holy Spirit, you will never know you have it. Don't you know that the child of God who has the baptism is inhabited by the Spirit? Remember the incident in the Bible where the Jews were going to stone Jesus? He slipped away from them, and shortly afterward, He healed the man with the blind eyes. (See John 8:48–9:7.) Slipping away from the crowd that was trying to kill Him, He showed forth His power.

Some people might think that Jesus should have run away altogether, but He stopped to heal. This thought has comforted me over and over again.

One day, as I was waiting for a streetcar, I stepped into a shoemaker's shop. I had not been there long when I saw a man with a green shade over his eyes. He was crying pitifully and was in great agony; it was heartbreaking. The shoemaker told me that the inflammation was intensely burning and injuring his eyes. I jumped up and went to the man and said, "You devil, come out of this man in the name of Jesus." Instantly, the man said, "It is all gone; I can see now." That is the only scriptural way: to begin to work at once, and to preach afterward. *"Jesus began both to do and teach"* (Acts 1:1).

GRACE ABOUNDING

You will find, as the days go by, that the miracles and healings will be manifested. Because the Master was *"touched with the feeling of* [the] *infirmities"* (Hebrews 4:15 KJV) of the multitudes, they instantly gathered around Him to hear what He had to say concerning the Word of God. However, I would rather see one man saved than ten thousand people healed. If you should ask me why, I would call your attention to the Word, which says, *"There was a certain rich man who…fared sumptuously every day"* (Luke 16:19). Now, we don't hear of this man having any diseases, but the Word says that, after he died, *"being in torments in Hades* ["hell," KJV], *he lifted up his eyes"* (Luke 16:23). We also read that there was a poor man who was full of sores, and that, after he died, he *"was carried by the angels to Abraham's bosom* [in heaven]" (verse 22). So we see that a man can die practically in good health, but be lost, and a man can die with disease and be saved; so it is more important to be saved than anything else.

But Jesus was sent to bear the infirmities and the afflictions of the people, and to *"destroy the works of the devil"* (1 John 3:8). He said, *"The thief [the devil] does not come except to steal, and to kill, and to destroy. I have come that they may have life, and that they may have it more abundantly"* (John 10:10). I maintain that God wishes all His people to have the more abundant life. We have the remedy for all sickness in the Word of God! Jesus paid the full price and the full redemption for every need, and where sin abounds, grace can come in and much more abound (see Romans 5:20), and dispel all the sickness.

When I was traveling by ship from England to Australia, I witnessed for Jesus, and it was not long before I had plenty of room to myself. If you want a whole seat to yourself, just begin to preach Jesus. However, some people listened and began to be much affected. One of the young men said to me, "I have never heard these truths before. You have so moved me that I must have a good conversation with you." The young man told me that his wife was a great believer in Christian Science, but that she was very sick now. Although she had tried everything, she had been unable to get relief, and so she was consulting a doctor. But the doctor gave her no hope whatsoever, and in her dilemma, and facing the reality of death, she asked that she might have an appointment with me.

When I went to see her in her cabin, I felt it would be unwise to say anything about Christian Science, so I said, "You are in bad shape." She said, "Yes, they give me no hope." I said, "I will not speak to you about anything, but will just lay my hands upon you in the name of Jesus, and when I do, you will be healed." That woke her up, and she began to think seriously. For three days, she was lamenting over the things she might have to give up. "Will I have to give up cigarettes?" "No," I said. "Will I have to give up dancing?" she asked.

And again I replied, "No." "Well, we do a little drinking sometimes and then we play cards also. Will I have to give—." "No," I said, "you will not have to give up anything. Only let us see Jesus." And right then she got such a vision of her crucified Savior, and Jesus was made so real to her, that she at once told her friends that she could not play cards anymore, could not drink or dance anymore, and that she would have to go back to England to preach against this awful thing, Christian Science. Oh, what a revelation Jesus gave her! Now, if I had refused to go when called for, saying that I first had to go to my cabin and pray about it, the Lord might have let that opportunity slip by. After you have received the Holy Spirit, you have power; you don't have to wait.

The other day, we were going through a very thickly populated part of San Francisco when we noticed that a large crowd had gathered. I saw it from the window of the streetcar I was riding in, and I said that I had to get out, which I did. There in the midst of the crowd was a boy in the agonies of death. As I threw my arms around the boy, I asked what the trouble was, and he answered that he had cramps. In the name of Jesus, I commanded the devils to come out of him, and at once he jumped up and, not even taking time to thank me, ran off perfectly healed. We are God's own children, quickened by His Spirit, and He has given us power over all the powers of darkness. (See Luke 10:19.) Christ in us is the open evidence of eternal glory. Christ in us is the Life, the Truth, and the Way. (See John 14:6.)

THE GREATNESS OF THE POWER

We have a wonderful salvation that fits everybody. I believe that a person who is baptized in the Holy Spirit has no conception of the power God has given him until he uses what he has. I maintain that

Peter and John had no idea of the greatness of the power they had, but they began to speculate. They said to the lame man who asked them for alms, "Well, as far as money goes, we have none of that, but we do have something; we don't exactly know what it is, but we will try it on you: *In the name of Jesus Christ of Nazareth, rise up and walk*" (Acts 3:6). And it worked. (See verses 1–10.)

In order to make yourself realize what you have in your possession, you will have to try it; and I can assure you, it will work all right. One time I said to a man that the Acts of the Apostles would never have been written if the apostles had not acted; and the Holy Spirit is still continuing His acts through us. May God help us to have some acts.

There is nothing like Pentecost, and if you have never been baptized in the Holy Spirit, you are making a big mistake by waiting. Don't you know that one of the main purposes for which God saved you was that you might bring salvation to others through Christ? For you to think that you have to remain stationary and just get to heaven is a great mistake. The baptism is to make you a witness for Jesus. The hardest way is the best way; you never hear anything about the person who is always having an easy time. The preachers always tell of how Moses crossed the Red Sea when he was at his wits' end. I cannot find a record of anyone in the Scriptures whom God used who was not first tried. So if you never have any trials, it is because you are not worth them.

God wants us to have power. When I was traveling on the train in Sweden early in the morning, a little lady and her daughter got onto the train at a certain station. I saw at once that the lady was in dreadful agony, and I asked my interpreter to inquire as to the trouble. With tears running down her face, she told how her daughter was taking her to the hospital to have her leg amputated. Everything possible had been done for her. I told her Jesus could heal. Just then the train stopped, and a crowd of people entered until there was hardly standing room; but friends, we never get into a place that is too awkward for God, though it seemed to me that the devil had sent these people in at that time to hinder her healing. However, when the train began to move along, I got down, although it was terribly crowded, and, putting my hands upon the woman's leg, I prayed for her in the name of Jesus. At once, she said to her daughter, "I am healed. It is all different now; I felt the power go down my leg." And she began to walk around. Then the train stopped at the next station, and this woman got out and walked up and down the platform, saying, "I am healed. I am healed."

Jesus was the *"firstfruits"* (1 Corinthians 15:20), and God has chosen us in Christ and has revealed His Son in us so that we might manifest Him in power. God gives us power over the devil, and when I say the devil, I mean everything that is not of God. Some people say we can afford to do without the baptism in the Spirit, but I say we cannot. I believe that any person who thinks there is a stop between Calvary and the glory has made a big mistake.

6

The Power of the Gospel

I am convinced that there is nothing in the world that is going to persuade men and women of the power of the Gospel like the manifestation of the Spirit with the fruits. God has baptized us in the Holy Spirit for a purpose: that He may show His mighty power in human flesh, as He did in Jesus. He is bringing us to a place where He may manifest these gifts.

JESUS IS THE WORD

"No one speaking by the Spirit of God calls Jesus accursed, and no one can say that Jesus is Lord except by the Holy Spirit" (1 Corinthians 12:3). Everyone who does not speak the truth concerning this Word, which is Jesus, makes Him the accursed; so all we have to do is to have the revelation of the Word in our hearts, and there will be no fear of our being led astray, because this Word is nothing else but Jesus.

In the gospel of John, we read that *"the Word was God"* (John 1:1), and that He *"became flesh and dwelt among us, and we beheld His glory, the glory as of the only begotten [Son] of the Father"* (verse 14). So it is revealed that He is the Son of God—the Word of God. The Bible is nothing else than the Word of God, and you can know right away—without getting mixed up at all—that everything that does not confess it is not of the Holy Spirit, and consequently you can wipe out all such things. There is no difficulty about saving yourselves, because the Word of God will always save.

WE RECEIVE THE ANOINTING OF THE HOLY ONE

There are diversities of gifts, but the same Spirit. There are differences of ministries, but the same Lord. And there are diversities of activities, but it is the same God who works all in all. But the manifestation of the Spirit is given to each one for the profit of all.   (1 Corinthians 12:4–7)

My heart is in this business. I am brought face-to-face with the fact that now the Holy Spirit is dwelling within me, that He is dwelling in my body; as John said, the anointing of the Holy One is within. (See 1 John 2:20.) The anointing of the Holy One is the Holy Spirit manifested in us. So we see that right away, within us, there is the power to manifest and bring forth those gifts that He has promised; and these gifts will be manifested in the measure that we live in the anointing of the Spirit of God. Thus we will find out that those gifts must be manifested.

My brother here, Mr. Moser, was suffering from lack of sleep. He had not had a full night of sleep for a long time. Last night I said, "I command you, in the name of Jesus, to sleep." When he came this morning, he was well; he had had a good night's sleep.

THE GIFTS ARE FOR THE PROFIT OF ALL

Beloved, the power of the Holy Spirit is within us *"for the profit of all"* (1 Corinthians 12:7). The Holy Spirit says in the Scriptures,

> *To one is given the word of wisdom through the Spirit, to another the word of knowledge through the same Spirit, to another faith by the same Spirit, to another gifts of healings by the same Spirit, to another the working of miracles, to another prophecy, to another discerning of spirits, to another different kinds of tongues, to another the interpretation of tongues. But one and the same Spirit works all these things, distributing to each one individually as He wills.* (1 Corinthians 12:8–11)

Paul distinctly said that it is possible for a person not to *"come short"* (1 Corinthains 1:7) in any gift, according to the measure of faith that he receives from the Lord Jesus. (See verses 4–9.) No doubt, some of you have sometimes thought what a blessed thing it would be if you had been the Virgin Mary. Listen, a certain woman said to Jesus, *"Blessed is the womb that bore You, and the breasts which nursed You!"* (Luke 11:27). But He answered, *"More than that, blessed are those who hear the word of God and keep it!"* (verse 28).

You see that a higher position than Mary's is attained through simple faith in what the Scriptures say. If we receive the Word of God as it is given to us, there will be power in our bodies to claim the gifts of God, and it will amaze the world when they see the power of God manifested through these gifts.

I believe that we are coming to a time when these gifts will be more distinctly manifested. What can be more convincing? Yes, He is a lovely Jesus. He went forth from place to place, rebuking demons, healing the sick, and doing other wonderful things. What was the reason? *"God was with Him"* (Acts 10:38).

Wherever there is a child of God who dares to receive the Word of God and cherish it, there God is made manifest in the flesh, for the Word of God is life and spirit (see John 6:63), and brings us into a place where we know that we have power with God and with men, in proportion to our loyalty of faith in the Word of God.

Now, beloved, I feel somehow that we have missed the greatest principle that underlies the baptism in the Holy Spirit. The greatest principle is that God the Holy Spirit came into our bodies to manifest the mighty works of God, *"for the profit of all"* (1 Corinthians 12:7). He does not manifest only one gift, but as God the Holy Spirit abides in my body, I find that He fills it, and then one can truly say that it is the anointing of the Holy One. It so fills us that we feel we can command demons to come out of those who are possessed; and when I lay hands on the sick in the name of the Lord Jesus, I realize that my body is merely the outer coil, and that within is the Son of God. For I receive the word of Christ, and Christ is in me, the power of God is in me. The Holy Spirit is making that word a living word, and the Holy Spirit makes me say, "Come out!" It is not Wigglesworth. It is the power of the Holy Spirit that manifests the glorious presence of Christ.

Smith Wigglesworth on the Holy Spirit

7

The Baptism in the Holy Spirit

How glad I am that God has baptized me in the Holy Spirit. What a wonderful difference it has made in my life. God has not promised that as Christians we will always feel very wonderful, but He has promised that if we stand on His Word, He will make His Word real in our lives. First we exercise faith; then it becomes fact. However, there are plenty of feelings in the fact, I assure you. God fills us with His own precious joy.

Samson is recorded in the eleventh chapter of Hebrews as being a man of faith. He was a man who was chosen by God from his mother's womb, but the power of God came upon him only on certain occasions. Yet we who have received the fullness of the Holy Spirit, the Comforter, may now have the anointing that abides forever.

The Lord has promised that we will have life and have it abundantly. (See John 10:10.) Look at the fifth chapter of Romans and see how many times the expression *"much more"* is used. (See, for example, Romans 5:9.) Oh, that we might take this abundant grace of God, revel in the Word of God, and be so full of expectancy that we will have this *"much more"* manifested as fruit in our lives.

THE FULLNESS OF THE SPIRIT

Some people realize that they have had the power of the Lord upon them and yet have failed to receive the fullness of the Spirit. Friend, what about you? God, in His love and kindness, has listed Samson in Hebrews 11 as an example for us. There came a time when, because of Samson's sin, his eyes were put out. His hair had been cut off, and he had lost his strength. He tried to break free of his bonds, but the Philistines got him. However, his hair grew again. The Philistines wanted him to entertain for them, but he prayed a prayer, and God answered. Oh, that we might turn to God and pray this prayer, as Samson did: *"O Lord God, remember me, I pray! Strengthen me, I pray, just this once, O God"* (Judges 16:28). God is *"plenteous in mercy"* (Psalm 86:5 KJV), and if you will turn to Him with true repentance, He will forgive you. Repentance means getting back to God.

When Samson took hold of the pillars upon which the Philistine house stood, he pulled the walls down. (See Judges 16:29–30). God can give you strength, and you can get hold of the posts, and He will work through you. No matter what kind of a backslider you have been, there is power in the blood. *"The blood of Jesus Christ His Son cleanses us from all sin"* (1 John 1:7). Oh, if I could only tell you how God so wonderfully restored me! I returned to my *"first love"* (Revelation 2:4), and He filled me with the Holy Spirit.

I want to draw your attention to a few verses from the second chapter of the Acts of the Apostles:

When the Day of Pentecost had fully come, they were all with one accord in one place. And suddenly there came a sound from heaven, as of a rushing mighty wind, and it filled the whole house where they were sitting. Then there appeared to them divided tongues, as of fire, and one sat upon each of them. And they were all filled with the Holy Spirit and began to speak with other tongues, as the Spirit gave them utterance. (Acts 2:1–4)

What a wonderful, divine position God intends us all to have, to be filled with the Holy Spirit. It is something so remarkable, so divine; it is, as it were, a great open door into all the treasury of the Most High. As the Spirit comes like *"rain upon the mown grass"* (Psalm 72:6 KJV), He turns the barrenness into greenness and freshness and life. Oh, hallelujah! God wants you to know that there is a place you may come to, in which you are dispensed with and God comes to be your assurance and sustaining power spiritually—until your dryness is turned into springs, until your barrenness becomes floods, until your whole life becomes vitalized by heaven, until heaven sweeps through you and dwells within you and turns everything inside out, until you are so absolutely filled with divine possibilities that you begin to live as a new creation. The Spirit of the living God sweeps through all weaknesses.

Beloved, God the Holy Spirit wants to bring us to a great revelation of life. He wants us to be filled with all the fullness of God. One of the most beautiful pictures we have in the Scriptures is of the Trinity. The Trinity was made manifest right on the banks of the Jordan River when Jesus was baptized. I want you to see how God unfolded heaven and how heaven and earth became the habitation of the Trinity. The voice of God came from the heavens as He looked at His well-beloved Son coming out of the waters, and there the Spirit was manifested in the shape of a dove. The dove is the only bird without gall; it is a creature so timid that at the least thing it moves and is afraid. No person can be baptized with the Holy Spirit and have bitterness, that is, gall.

A DOUBLE CURE

My friend, you need a double cure. You first need saving and cleansing and then the baptism of the Holy Spirit, until the old man never rises anymore, until you are absolutely dead to sin and alive to God by His Spirit and know that old things have passed away. When the Holy Spirit gets possession of a person, he is a new man entirely—his whole being becomes saturated with divine power. We become a habitation of Him who is all light, all revelation, all power, and all love. Yes, God the Holy Spirit is manifested within us in such a way that it is glorious.

There was a certain rich man in London whose business flourished. He used to count all his many assets, but he was still troubled inside; he didn't know what to do. Walking around his large building, he came upon a boy who was the doorkeeper and found the boy whistling. Looking at him, he sized up the whole situation completely and went back to his office again and puzzled over the matter. He went back to his business but he could find no peace. His bank could not help him; his money, his success, could not help him. He had an aching void. He was helpless within. My friend, having the world without having God is like being a whitewashed sepulcher. (See Matthew 23:27.)

When he could get no rest, he exclaimed, "I will go and see what the boy is doing." Again he went and found him whistling. "I want you to come into my office," he said. When they entered the office, the man said, "Tell me, what makes you so happy and cheerful?" "Oh," replied the boy, "I used to be so miserable until I went to a little mission and heard about Jesus. Then I was saved and filled with the Holy Spirit. I am always whistling inside; if I am not whistling, I am singing. I am just full!"

This rich man obtained the address of the mission from the boy, went to the services, and sat beside the door. But the power of God moved so strongly that when the altar call was given, he responded. God saved him and, a few days afterward, filled him with the Holy Spirit. The man found himself at his desk, shouting, "Oh, hallelujah!"

I know the Lord, I know the Lord,
I know the Lord's laid His hand on me.
I know the Lord, I know the Lord,
I know the Lord's laid His hand on me.

Oh, this blessed Son of God wants to fill us with such glory until our whole body is aflame with the power of the Holy Spirit. I see there is *"much more"* (Romans 5:9). Glory to God! My daughter asked some African boys to tell us the difference between being saved and being filled with the Holy Spirit. "Ah," they said, "when we were saved, it was very good; but when we received the Holy Spirit, it was more so." Many of you have never received the "more so."

After the Holy Spirit comes upon you, you will have power. God will mightily move within your life; the power of the Holy Spirit will overshadow you, inwardly moving you until you know there is a divine plan different from anything that you have had in your life before.

Has He come? He is going to come to you. I am expecting that God will so manifest His presence and power that He will show you the necessity of receiving the Holy Spirit. Also, God will heal the people who need healing. Everything is to be had now: salvation, sanctification, the fullness of the Holy Spirit, and healing. God is working mightily by the power of His Spirit, bringing to us a fullness of His perfect redemption until every soul may know that God has all power.

8

Clothed in the Spirit

God has a plan for us in this life of the Spirit, this abundant life. Jesus came so that we might have life. (See John 10:10.) Satan comes to steal and kill and destroy (see verse 10), but God has abundance for us—full measure, pressed down, shaken together, overflowing, abundant measure. (See Luke 6:38.) This abundance is God filling us with His own personality and presence, making us salt and light and giving us a revelation of Himself. It is God with us in all circumstances, afflictions, persecutions, and trials, girding us with truth. Christ the Initiative, the Triune God, is in control, and our every thought, word, and action must be in line with Him, with no weakness or failure. Our God is a God of might, light, and revelation, preparing us for heaven. Our lives are *"hidden with Christ in God"* (Colossians 3:3). When He who is our life is manifested, we will also *"appear with Him in glory"* (verse 4).

THE GUARANTEE OF THE SPIRIT

For we know that if our earthly house, this tent, is destroyed, we have a building from God, a house not made with hands, eternal in the heavens....For we who are in this tent groan, being burdened, not because we want to be unclothed, but further clothed, that mortality may be swallowed up by life. Now He who has prepared us for this very thing is God, who also has given us the Spirit as a guarantee. (2 Corinthians 5:1, 4–5)

God's Word is a tremendous word, a productive word. It produces what it is—power. It produces Godlikeness. We get to heaven through Christ, the Word of God; we have peace through the blood of His cross. Redemption is ours through the knowledge of the Word. I am saved because God's Word says so: *"If you confess with your mouth the Lord Jesus and believe in your heart that God has raised Him from the dead, you will be saved"* (Romans 10:9).

If I am baptized with the Holy Spirit, it is because Jesus said, *"You shall receive power when the Holy Spirit has come upon you"* (Acts 1:8). We must all have one thought—to be filled with the Holy Spirit, to be filled with God.

INTERPRETATION OF TONGUES

God has sent His Word to free us from the "law of sin and death." Except we die, we cannot live; except we cease to be, God cannot be.

The Holy Spirit has a royal plan, a heavenly plan. He came to unveil the King, to show the character of God, to unveil the precious blood of Jesus. Because I have the Holy Spirit within me, I see Jesus clothed for humanity. He was moved by the Spirit, led by the Spirit.

We read of some who heard the Word of God but did not benefit from it because faith was lacking in them. (See Hebrews 4:2.) We must have a living faith in God's Word, a faith that is quickened by the Spirit.

A man may be saved and still be carnally minded. When many people hear about the baptism of the Holy Spirit, their carnal minds at once arise against the Holy Spirit. *"The carnal mind…is not subject to the law of God, nor indeed can be"* (Romans 8:7). One time, Jesus' disciples wanted to call down fire from heaven as a punishment against a Samaritan village for not welcoming Him. But Jesus said to them, *"You do not know what manner of spirit you are of"* (Luke 9:55).

> *For we who are in this tent groan, being burdened, not because we want to be unclothed, but further clothed, that mortality may be swallowed up by life. Now He who has prepared us for this very thing is God, who also has given us the Spirit as a guarantee.* (2 Corinthians 5:4–5)

When we are clothed with the Spirit, our human depravity is covered and everything that is contrary to the mind of God is destroyed. God must have people for Himself who are being clothed with a heavenly habitation, perfectly prepared by the Holy Spirit for the Day of the Lord. *"For in this we groan, earnestly desiring to be clothed with our habitation which is from heaven"* (verse 2).

Was Paul speaking here only about the coming of the Lord? No. Yet this condition of preparedness on earth is related to our heavenly state. The Holy Spirit is coming to take out of the world a church that is a perfect bride. He must find in us perfect yieldedness, with every desire subjected to Him. He has come to reveal Christ in us so that the glorious flow of the life of God may flow out of us, bringing rivers of living water to the thirsty land.

"If Christ is in you, the body is dead because of sin, but the Spirit is life because of righteousness" (Romans 8:10).

THE PLAN OF THE SPIRIT

INTERPRETATION OF TONGUES

This is what God has declared: freedom from the law. "If we love the world, the love of the Father is not in us."

For all that is in the world; the lust of the flesh, the lust of the eyes, and the pride of life; is not of the Father but is of the world.
(1 John 2:16)

The Spirit has to breathe into us a new occupancy, a new order. He came to give the vision of a life in which Jesus is perfected in us.

[God] *has saved us and called us with a holy calling, not according to our works, but according to His own purpose and grace which was given to us in Christ Jesus before time began, but has now been revealed by the appearing of our Savior Jesus Christ, who has abolished death and brought life and immortality to light through the gospel.* (2 Timothy 1:9–10)

We are saved, called with a holy calling—called to be saints, holy, pure, Godlike, sons with power. It has been a long time now since the debt of sin was settled, our redemption was secured, and death was abolished. Mortality is a hindrance, but death no longer has power. Sin no longer has dominion. You reign in Christ; you appropriate His finished work. Don't groan and travail for a week if you are in need; *"only believe"* (Mark 5:36). Don't fight to get some special thing; *"only believe."* It is according to your faith that you will receive. (See Matthew 9:29.) God blesses you with faith. *"Have faith in God"* (Mark 11:22). If you are free in God, believe, and it will come to pass.

"If then you were raised with Christ, seek those things which are above, where Christ is, sitting at the right hand of God" (Colossians 3:1). Stir yourselves up, beloved! Where are you? I have been planted with Christ in the likeness of His death, and I am risen with Christ. (See Romans 6:5) It was a beautiful planting. I am seated with Him in heavenly places. (See Ephesians 2:6.) God credits me with righteousness through faith in Christ (see Romans 4:5), and I believe Him. Why should I doubt?

INTERPRETATION OF TONGUES

Why do you doubt? Faith reigns. God makes it possible. How many receive the Holy Spirit, and Satan gets a doubt in? Don't doubt; believe. There is power and strength in Him; who will dare to believe God?

Leave Doubting Street; live on Faith-Victory Street. Jesus sent the seventy out, and they came back in victory. (See Luke 10:1–18.) It takes God to make it real. Dare to believe until there is not a sick person, until there is no sickness, until everything that is not of God is withered, and the life of Jesus is implanted within.

9

New Wine

It is a settled thing in the glory that in the fullness of time the latter rain has to be greater than the former. (See Zechariah 10:1; James 5:7.) Some of our hearts have been greatly moved by the former rain, but it is the latter rain we are crying out for. What will it be like when the fullness comes and the heart of God is satisfied?

On the Day of Pentecost, *"they were all filled with the Holy Spirit and began to speak with other tongues, as the Spirit gave them utterance"* (Acts 2:4). What a lovely thought that the Holy Spirit had such sway that the words were all His! We are having to learn, whether we like it or not, that our end is God's beginning. Then it is all God; the Lord Jesus stands forth in the midst with such divine glory, and men are impelled, filled, led so perfectly. Nothing else will meet the need of the world.

We see that there was something beautiful about Peter and John when we read that people *"realized that they had been with Jesus"* (Acts 4:13). There was something so real, so after the order of the Master, about them.

> *Now when they saw the boldness of Peter and John, and perceived that they were uneducated and untrained men, they marveled. And they realized that they had been with Jesus.*
>
> (verse 13)

May all in the temple glorify Jesus; it can be so.

The one thing that was more marked than anything else in the life of Jesus was the fact that the people glorified God in Him. And when God is glorified and gets the right-of-way and the wholehearted attention of His people, everyone is as He is, filled with God. Whatever it costs, it must be. Let it be so. Filled with God! The only thing that will help people is to speak the latest thing God has given us from the glory.

There is nothing outside salvation. We are filled, immersed, clothed upon with the Spirit. There must be nothing felt, seen, or spoken about except the mighty power of the Holy Spirit. We are new creatures in Christ Jesus, baptized into a new nature. *"He who believes in Me, as the Scripture has said, out of his heart will flow rivers of living water"* (John 7:38). The very life of the risen Christ is to be in everything we are and do, moving us to do His will.

There is something we have not yet touched in the spiritual realm, but praise God for the thirst to be in this meeting! Praise God, the thirst is of God, the desire is of God, the plan is of God, the purpose is of God. It is God's plan, God's thought, God's vessel, and God's servant. We are in the world to meet the need, but we are not of the world or of its spirit. (See John 17:15–16.)

We are *"partakers of the divine nature"* (2 Peter 1:4) to manifest the life of Jesus to the world. This is God incarnate in humanity.

On the Day of Pentecost, *"others mocking said, 'They are full of new wine'"* (Acts 2:13). That is what we want, you say? *"New wine"*—a new order, a new inspiration, a new manifestation. New, new, new, new wine. A power all new in itself, as if you were born, as you are, into a new day, a new creation. *"No man ever spoke like this Man!"* (John 7:46).

This new wine has a freshness about it! It has a beauty about it! It has a quality about it! It creates in others the desire for the same taste. At Pentecost, some saw, but three thousand felt, tasted, and enjoyed. Some looked on; others drank with a new faith never before seen—a new manifestation, a new realization all divine, a new thing. It came straight from heaven, from the throne of the glorified Lord. It is God's purpose to fill us with that wine, to make us ready to burst forth with new rivers, with fresh energy, with no tired feeling.

God manifested in the flesh. That is what we want, and it is what God wants, and it satisfies everybody. All the people said, "We have never seen anything like it." (See Acts 2:7–12.) The disciples rejoiced in its being new; others were *"cut to the heart, [crying out] to Peter and the rest of the apostles, 'Men and brethren, what shall we do?'"* (verse 37).

Then Peter said to them, "Repent, and let every one of you be baptized in the name of Jesus Christ for the remission of sins; and you shall receive the gift of the Holy Spirit. For the promise is to you and to your children, and to all who are afar off, as many as the Lord our God will call." And with many other words he testified and exhorted them, saying, "Be saved from this perverse generation."   (verses 38–40)

What shall we do? Men and brethren, what shall we do? Believe! Stretch out! Press on! Let there be a new entering in, a new passion to have it. We must be beside ourselves; we must drink deeply of the new wine so that multitudes may be satisfied and find satisfaction too.

The new wine must have a new wineskin—that is the necessity of a new vessel. (See Matthew 9:17.) If anything of the old is left, not put to death, destroyed, there will be a tearing and a breaking. The new wine and the old vessel will not work in harmony. It must be new wine and a new wineskin. Then there will be nothing to discard when Jesus comes.

> *For the Lord Himself will descend from heaven with a shout, with the voice of an archangel, and with the trumpet of God. And the dead in Christ will rise first. Then we who are alive and remain shall be caught up together with them in the clouds to meet the Lord in the air. And thus we shall always be with the Lord.*   (1 Thessalonians 4:16–17)

The Spirit is continually working within us to change us until the day when we will be like Him:

> [The Lord Jesus Christ] *will transform our lowly body that it may be conformed to His glorious body, according to the working by which He is able even to subdue all things to Himself.*
>   (Philippians 3:21)

I desire that all of you be so filled with the Spirit, so hungry, so thirsty, that nothing will satisfy you but seeing Jesus. We are to get more thirsty every day, more dry every day, until the floods come and the Master passes by, ministering to us and through us the same life, the same inspiration, so that *"as He is, so are we in this world"* (1 John 4:17).

When Jesus became the sacrifice for man, He was in great distress, but it was accomplished. It meant strong crying and tears (see Hebrews 5:7); it meant the cross manward but the glory heavenward. Glory descending on a cross! Truly, *"great is the mystery of godliness"* (1 Timothy 3:16). He cried, *"It is finished!"* (John 19:30). Let the cry never be stopped until the heart of Jesus is satisfied, until His plan for humanity is reached in the sons of God being manifested (see Romans 8:19) and in the earth being *"filled with the knowledge of the glory of the LORD, as the waters cover the sea"* (Habakkuk 2:14). Amen. Amen. Amen.

Smith Wigglesworth on Healing

10

He Himself Took Our Infirmities

And He cast out the spirits with a word, and healed all who were sick, that it might be fulfilled which was spoken by Isaiah the prophet, saying: "He Himself took our infirmities and bore our sicknesses." (Matthew 8:16–17)

Here we have a wonderful word. All of the Word is wonderful. This blessed Book brings such life, health, peace, and abundance that we should never be poor anymore. This Book is my heavenly bank. I find everything I want in it. I desire to show you how rich you may be, so that in everything you can be enriched in Christ Jesus. (See 1 Corinthians 1:5.) For you He has *"abundance of grace and… the gift of righteousness"* (Romans 5:17), and through His abundant grace *"all things are possible"* (Matthew 19:26). I want to show you that you can be a living branch of the living Vine, Christ Jesus, and that it is your privilege to be, right here in this world, what He is.

John told us, "*As He is, so are we in this world*" (1 John 4:17). Not that we are anything in ourselves, but Christ within us is our All in All.

The Lord Jesus is always wanting to show forth His grace and love in order to draw us to Himself. God is willing to do things, to manifest His Word, and to let us know a measure of the mind of our God in this day and hour.

A LEPER IS MIRACULOUSLY CLEANSED

Today there are many needy ones, many afflicted ones, but I do not think anyone present is half as bad as this first case that we read of in Matthew 8:

> *When He had come down from the mountain, great multitudes followed Him. And behold, a leper came and worshiped Him, saying, "Lord, if You are willing, You can make me clean." Then Jesus put out His hand and touched him, saying, "I am willing; be cleansed." Immediately his leprosy was cleansed. And Jesus said to him, "See that you tell no one; but go your way, show yourself to the priest, and offer the gift that Moses commanded, as a testimony to them."* (Matthew 8:1–4)

This man was a leper. You may be suffering from tuberculosis, cancer, or other things, but God will show forth His perfect cleansing, His perfect healing, if you have a living faith in Christ. He is a wonderful Jesus.

This leper must have been told about Jesus. How much is missed because people are not constantly telling what Jesus will do in our day. Probably someone had come to that leper and said, "Jesus can heal you." So he was filled with expectation as he saw the Lord coming down the mountainside. Lepers were not allowed to come within reach of people; they were shut out as unclean. Ordinarily, it would have been very difficult for him to get near because of the crowd that surrounded Jesus. But as Jesus came down from the mountain, He met the leper; He came to the leper.

Oh, leprosy is a terrible disease! There was no help for him, humanly speaking, but nothing is too hard for Jesus. The man cried, *"Lord, if You are willing, You can make me clean"* (Matthew 8:2). Was Jesus willing? You will never find Jesus missing an opportunity to do good. You will find that He is always more willing to work than we are to give Him an opportunity to work. The trouble is that we do not come to Him; we do not ask Him for what He is more than willing to give.

"Then Jesus put out His hand and touched him, saying, 'I am willing; be cleansed.' Immediately his leprosy was cleansed" (verse 3). I like that. If you are definite with Him, you will never go away disappointed. The divine life will flow into you, and instantaneously you will be delivered. This Jesus is just the same today, and He says to you, "I am willing; be cleansed." He has an overflowing cup for you, a fullness of life. He will meet you in your absolute helplessness. All things are possible if you will only believe. (See Mark 9:23.) God has a real plan. It is very simple: just come to Jesus. You will find Him just the same as He was in days of old. (See Hebrews 13:8.)

JESUS HEALS BY SAYING A WORD

The next case we have in Matthew 8 is that of the centurion coming and pleading with Jesus on behalf of his servant, who was paralyzed and was dreadfully tormented.

Now when Jesus had entered Capernaum, a centurion came to Him, pleading with Him, saying, "Lord, my servant is lying at home paralyzed, dreadfully tormented." And Jesus said to him, "I will come and heal him." The centurion answered and said, "Lord, I am not worthy that You should come under my roof. But only speak a word, and my servant will be healed. For I also am a man under authority, having soldiers under me. And I say to this one, 'Go,' and he goes; and to another, 'Come,' and he comes; and to my servant, 'Do this,' and he does it." When Jesus heard it, He marveled, and said to those who followed, "Assuredly, I say to you, I have not found such great faith, not even in Israel! And I say to you that many will come from east and west, and sit down with Abraham, Isaac, and Jacob in the kingdom of heaven. But the sons of the kingdom will be cast out into outer darkness. There will be weeping and gnashing of teeth." Then Jesus said to the centurion, "Go your way; and as you have believed, so let it be done for you." And his servant was healed that same hour. (Matthew 8:5–13)

This man was so earnest that he came seeking Jesus. Notice that there is one thing certain: there is no such thing as seeking without finding. *"He who seeks finds"* (Matthew 7:8). Listen to the gracious words of Jesus: *"I will come and heal him"* (Matthew 8:7).

In most places where I go, there are many people whom I cannot pray for. In some places there are two or three hundred people who would like me to visit them, but I am not able to do so. Yet I am glad that the Lord Jesus is always willing to come and heal. He longs to help the sick ones. He loves to heal them of their afflictions. The Lord is healing many people today by means of handkerchiefs, even as He did in the days of Paul. (See Acts 19:11–12.)

A woman came to me in the city of Liverpool and said, "I would like you to help me by joining me in prayer. My husband is a drunkard and every night comes into the home under the influence of drink. Won't you join me in prayer for him?" I asked the woman, "Do you have a handkerchief?" She took out a handkerchief, and I prayed over it and told her to lay it on the pillow of the drunken man. He came home that night and laid his head on the pillow in which this handkerchief was tucked. He laid his head on more than the pillow that night, for he laid his head on the promise of God. In Mark 11:24, we read, *"Whatever things you ask when you pray, believe that you receive them, and you will have them."*

The next morning the man got up and, going into the first saloon that he had to pass on his way to work, ordered some beer. He tasted it and said to the bartender, "You put some poison in this beer." He could not drink it and went on to the next saloon and ordered some more beer. He tasted it and said to the man behind the counter, "You put some poison in this beer. I believe you folks have plotted to poison me." The bartender was indignant at being charged with this crime. The man said, "I will go somewhere else." He went to another saloon, and the same thing happened as in the two previous saloons. He made such a fuss that he was thrown out.

After he left work that evening, he went to another saloon to get some beer, and again he thought the bartender was trying to poison him. Again, he made such a disturbance that he was thrown out. He went to his home and told his wife what had happened and said, "It seems as though all the fellows have agreed to poison me." His wife said to him, "Can't you see the hand of the Lord in this, that He is making you dislike the stuff that has been your ruin?" This word brought conviction to the man's heart, and he came to the meeting and got saved. The Lord still has power to set the captives free.

Jesus was willing to go and heal the sick servant, but the centurion said, *"Lord, I am not worthy that You should come under my roof. But only speak a word, and my servant will be healed"* (Matthew 8:8). Jesus was delighted with this expression and *"said to the centurion, 'Go your way; and as you have believed, so let it be done for you.' And his servant was healed that same hour"* (verse 13).

FACING A DEMON-POSSESSED WOMAN

I received a telegram once urging me to visit a case about two hundred miles from my home. As I went to this place, I met the father and mother and found them brokenhearted. They led me up a staircase to a room, and I saw a young woman on the floor. Five men were holding her down. She was a frail young woman, but the power in her was greater than the strength of all those young men. As I went into the room, the evil powers looked out of her eyes, and they used her lips, saying, "We are many; you can't cast us out." I said, "Jesus can."

Jesus is equal to every occasion. He is waiting for an opportunity to bless. He is ready for every opportunity to deliver souls. When we receive Jesus, the following verse is true of us: *"Greater is he that is in [us], than he that is in the world"* (1 John 4:4 KJV). He is greater than all the powers of darkness. No man can meet the devil in his own strength, but any man filled with the knowledge of Jesus, filled with His presence, filled with His power, is more than a match for the powers of darkness. God has called us to be *"more than conquerors through Him who loved us"* (Romans 8:37).

The living Word is able to destroy satanic forces. There is power in the name of Jesus. My desire is that every window on the street have the name of Jesus written on it.

Through faith in His name, deliverance was brought to this poor bound soul, and thirty-seven demons came out, giving their names as they came forth. The dear woman was completely delivered, and the family was able to give her back her child. That night there was heaven in that home, and the father, mother, son, and his wife were all united in glorifying Christ for His infinite grace. The next morning we had a gracious time in the breaking of bread.

All things are wonderful with our wonderful Jesus. If you would dare rest your all upon Him, things would take place, and He would change the whole situation. In a moment, through the name of Jesus, a new order of things can be brought in.

In the world, new diseases are always surfacing, and the doctors cannot identify them. A doctor said to me, "The science of medicine is in its infancy, and we doctors really have no confidence in our medicine. We are always experimenting." But the man of God does not experiment. He knows, or ought to know, redemption in its fullness. He knows, or ought to know, the mightiness of the Lord Jesus Christ. He is not, or should not, be moved by outward observation but should get a divine revelation of the mightiness of the name of Jesus and the power of His blood. If we exercise our faith in the Lord Jesus Christ, He will come forth and get glory over all the powers of darkness.

CHRIST BORE OUR SICKNESS AND SIN

When evening had come, they brought to Him many who were demon-possessed. And He cast out the spirits with a word, and healed all who were sick, that it might be fulfilled which was spoken by Isaiah the prophet, saying: "He Himself took our infirmities and bore our sicknesses." (Matthew 8:16–17)

The work is done if you only believe it. It is done. "He Himself took our infirmities and bore our sicknesses." If only you can see the Lamb of God going to Calvary! He took our flesh so that He could take upon Himself the full burden of all our sin and all the consequences of sin. There on the cross of Calvary, the results of sin were also dealt with.

> *Inasmuch then as the children have partaken of flesh and blood, He Himself likewise shared in the same, that through death He might destroy him who had the power of death, that is, the devil, and release those who through fear of death were all their lifetime subject to bondage.* (Hebrews 2:14–15)

Through His death there is deliverance for you today.

11

Divine Life Brings Divine Health

See from Mark 1 how Jesus was quickened by the power of the Spirit of God and how He was driven by the Spirit into the wilderness. (See verses 9–12.) See how John also was so filled with the Spirit of God that he had a "cry" within him, and the cry moved all Israel. (See verses 2–5). When God gets hold of a man in the Spirit, he can have a new cry—something in God's order. A man may cry for fifty years without the Spirit of the Lord, and the more he cries, the less people notice him. But if he is filled with the Holy Spirit and cries once, people feel the effects.

ENERGIZED BY THE SPIRIT

So there is a necessity for every one of us to be filled with God. It is not sufficient to have just a touch or to be filled with just a desire. Only one thing will meet the needs of the people, and that is for you to be immersed in the life of God. This means that God takes you and fills you with His Spirit until you live right in God. He does this so that *"whether you eat or drink, or whatever you do, [it may be] all to the glory of God"* (1 Corinthians 10:31). In that place you will find that all your strength and all your mind and all your soul are filled with a zeal, not only for worship, but for proclamation. This proclamation is accompanied by all the power of God, which must move satanic power and disturb the world.

The reason the world is not seeing Jesus is that Christian people are not filled with Jesus. They are satisfied with attending meetings weekly, reading the Bible occasionally, and praying sometimes. Beloved, if God lays hold of you by the Spirit, you will find that there is an end of everything and a beginning of God. Your whole body will become seasoned with a divine likeness of God. Not only will He have begun to use you, but He will have taken you in hand, so that you might be *"a vessel for honor"* (2 Timothy 2:21). Our lives are not to be for ourselves, for if we live for ourselves we will die (see Romans 8:13); but if *"by the Spirit [we] put to death the deeds of the body, [we] will live"* (verse 13). He who lives in the Spirit is subject to the powers of God, but he who lives for himself will die. The man who lives in the Spirit lives a life of freedom and joy and blessing and service—a life that brings blessing to others. God would have us see that we must live in the Spirit.

YOU CAN BE LIKE JESUS

In Mark 1, we have two important factors in the Spirit. One is Jesus filled with the Holy Spirit and driven by the Spirit's power. The other is John the Baptist, who was so filled with the Spirit of God that his one aim was to go out preaching. We find him in the wilderness. What a strange place to be! Beloved, it was quite natural for Jesus, after He had served a whole day among the multitudes, to want to go to His Father and pray all night. Why? He wanted a source of strength and power; He wanted an association with His Father that would bring everything else to a place of submission.

After Jesus had been on the mountain communing with His Father and after He had been clothed with God's holy presence and Spirit, when He met the demon power, it had to go. (See Matthew 17:1–9, 14–18.) When He met sickness, it had to leave. He came from the mountain with power to meet whatever needs the people had.

I do not know what your state of grace is—whether you are saved or not—but it is an awful thing for me to see people who profess to be Christians lifeless, powerless, and in a place where their lives are so parallel to unbelievers' lives that it is difficult to tell which place they are in, whether in the flesh or in the Spirit. Many people live in the place that is described to us by Paul in Romans 7:25: *"With the mind I myself serve the law of God, but with the flesh the law of sin."* That is the place where sin is in the ascendancy. But when the power of God comes to you, it is to separate you from yourself. It is destruction of yourself, annihilation. It is to move you from nature to grace, making you mighty over the powers of the Enemy and making you know that you have now begun to live a life of faith in the Son of God.

TURNING STRUGGLES INTO REST

I pray that God will give us a way out of difficulties and into rest. The writer to the Hebrews told us that *"there remains therefore a rest for the people of God"* (Hebrews 4:9). Those who have entered into that rest have ceased from their own works. (See verse 10.) Oh, what a blessed state of rest that is, to cease from your own works. There God is enthroned in your life, and you are working for Him by a new order. If you preach, you no longer struggle to preach in the old way of sermonettes. God wants to bring you forth as a flame of fire with a message from God, with a truth that will disturb the powers of Satan, and with an unlimited supply for every needy soul. Then, just as John moved all of Israel with a cry, you, by the power of the Holy Spirit, will move the people.

This is what Jesus meant when He said to Nicodemus,

> *Unless one is born again, he cannot see the kingdom of God. ...[For] that which is born of the flesh is flesh, and that which is born of the Spirit is spirit. Do not marvel that I said to you, "You must be born again."* (John 3:3, 6–7)

Oh, if you only knew what those words mean. To be born of God! It means no less than God being born anew in us—a new order of God; a new plan; a new faith by God; a new child of God; a new life from God; a new creation living in the world but not of the world, reigning in life over all the powers of the world, over whom *"sin shall not have dominion"* (Romans 6:14).

LIFE BY THE SPIRIT

How will we reach these beatitudes in the Spirit? How will we come into the presence of God? How will we attain to these divine principles? Beloved, it is not in the flesh and never was! How can it be, when the Scripture plainly says that if we live according to the flesh we will die? (See Romans 8:13.) But if we live *"by the Spirit,"* we will *"put to death the deeds of the body"* (verse 13) and will find that *"mortality [will] be swallowed up by life"* (2 Corinthians 5:4). Life will prevail in the body and in the mind, over self, over disease, over everything in the world, so that we may walk around without being distracted by any bodily ailments. Are we in this place?

I dare say that many of you are in a bound condition, with lots of things to remind you that you have a body. Do you not know that Jesus Christ was manifested to *"destroy the works of the devil"* (1 John 3:8), to loose you from the bondage of self, and to free you from the bondage of the present evil world? Do you not know that Jesus came for the express purpose of destroying the flesh?

Jesus proceeded from the Father and went to the Father. That blessed, blessed Jesus. Have you received Him? I have no doubt that if I were to ask you whether you believe in Jesus, many of you would say that you have believed in Jesus all your lives. But if I were to ask, "Are you saved?" many of you would unhesitatingly reply that you have never done anything wrong in your whole lives but have always done what is right and honorable. Oh, you hypocrites! You self-righteous vipers! There is no such person on the earth. "All *have sinned and fall short of the glory of God"* (Romans 3:23, emphasis added). How will we get rid of our sins? *"The blood of Jesus Christ His Son cleanses us from all sin"* (1 John 1:7). How will we get rid of our diseases? *"The blood of Jesus Christ His Son cleanses us from all* [diseases]." You cannot think about that blessed One without becoming holy.

We have a Scripture that says, *"Whatever is born of God overcomes the world…. Who is he who overcomes the world, but he who believes that Jesus is the Son of God?"* (1 John 5:4–5). The one who is born again overcomes the world, and if you find that the world overcomes you, you can be sure that you have never known this Jesus. Jesus *"was manifested…[to] destroy the works of the devil"* (1 John 3:8).

I want to talk until you are shaken and disturbed, until you see where you are. If I can get you to search the Scriptures after I leave this place and to see if I have been preaching according to the Word of God, then I will be pleased. Wake up to see that the Scriptures have life and freedom for you. They have nothing less than power to make you sons of God, free in the Holy Spirit.

Now Jesus came to bring back to us what was forfeited in the garden. Adam and Eve were there—free from sin and disease—and first sin came, then disease, and then death. People want to say this is not so! But I tell you, "Get the devil out of you, and you will have a different body. Get disease out, and you will get the devil out."

Jesus rebuked sickness, and it went. So this morning, I want to bring you to a place where you will see that you are healed. You must give God your life. You must see that sickness has to go and that God has to come in. You must see that your life has to be clean and that God will keep you holy. You must see that you have to walk before God and that He will make you perfect, for God says, *"Pursue...holiness, without which no one will see the Lord"* (Hebrews 12:14). Moreover, as *"we walk in the light as He is in the light, we have fellowship with one another, and the blood of Jesus Christ His Son cleanses us from all sin"* (1 John 1:7).

A PLACE OF VICTORY

I want to say to you believers that there is a very blessed place for you to attain to, and the place where God wants you is a place of victory. When the Spirit of the Lord comes into your life, there must be victory. The disciples, before they received the Holy Spirit, were always in bondage. Jesus said to them one day, just before the Crucifixion, *"One of you will betray Me"* (Matthew 26:21), and they were so conscious of their inability, helplessness, and human depravity that they said to Jesus, *"Is it I?"* (verse 22). Then Peter was ashamed that he had taken that stand, and he rose up and said, *"Even if all are made to stumble because of You, I will never be made to stumble*" (verse 33). Likewise, the others rose up and declared that neither would they (see verse 35), but every one of them did leave Him.

However, beloved, after they received the power of the outpouring of the Holy Spirit, they were made as bold as lions to meet any difficulty. They were made to stand any test. When the power of God fell upon them in the Upper Room, these same men who had failed before the Crucifixion came out in front of all those people who were gathered together and accused them of crucifying the Lord of Glory. They were bold. What had made them like this? Purity. I tell you, purity is bold. Take, for instance, a little child. He will gaze straight into your eyes for as long as you like, without looking away once. The purer a person is, the bolder he is. I tell you, God wants to bring us into that divine purity of heart and life, that holy boldness. Not arrogance, not big-headedness, not self-righteousness, but a pure, holy, divine appointment by One who will come in and live with you. He will defy the powers of Satan and put you in a place of victory, a place of overcoming the world.

You never inherited that kind of victory from the flesh. That is a gift from God, by the Spirit, to all who obey. Therefore, no one can say he wishes he were an overcomer but that he has failed and failed until he has no hope. Beloved, God can make *you* an overcomer. When the Spirit of God comes into your body, He transforms you; He gives you life. Oh, there is a life in the Spirit that makes you "*free from the law of sin and death*" (Romans 8:2) and gives you boldness and personality. It is the personality of the Deity. It is God in you.

I tell you that God is able to so transform you and bring you into order by the Spirit that you can become a new creation after God's order. There is no such thing as defeat for the believer. Without the

Cross, without Christ's righteousness, without the new birth, without the indwelling Christ, without this divine incoming of God, I see myself as a failure. But God the Holy Spirit can come in and take our place until we are renewed in righteousness, until we are made the children of God.

Do you think that God made you in order to watch you fail? God never made men in order to see them fail. He made men in order that they might be sons who walk the earth in power. So when I look at you, I know that God can give you the capability to bring everything into subjection. Yes, you can have the power of Christ dwelling in you. His power can bring every evil thing under your feet and make you master over the flesh and the devil. His power can work until nothing rises within you except what will magnify and glorify the Lord.

God wants me to show you Jesus' disciples, who were very frail like you and me, so that we, too, may now be filled with God and become ambassadors of this wonderful truth I am preaching. We see Peter, frail, helpless, and at every turn a failure. However, God filled that man with the Spirit of His righteousness until he went up and down as bold as a lion. Moreover, when he faced death—even crucifixion—he counted himself unworthy of being crucified like his Lord and asked that his murderers would put him upside down on the cross. He had a deep submissiveness and a power that was greater than all flesh. Peter had received the power of God.

GOD'S UNFAILING WORD

The Scriptures do not tell two different stories. They tell the truth. I want you to know the truth, *"and the truth shall make you free"* (John 8:32). What is truth? Jesus said, *"I am the way, the truth, and the life"* (John 14:6). He also said, *"He who believes in Me, as the*

Scripture has said, out of his heart will flow rivers of living water" (John 7:38). He said this concerning the Spirit, who would be given after Jesus had been glorified. (See verse 39.)

I find nothing in the Bible but holiness, and nothing in the world but worldliness. Therefore, if I live in the world, I will become worldly; on the other hand, if I live in the Bible, I will become holy. This is the truth, *"and the truth shall make you free"* (John 8:32).

GOD'S TRANSFORMING POWER

The power of God can remodel you. He can make you hate sin and love righteousness. (See Psalm 45:7.) He can take away bitterness and hatred and covetousness and malice. He can so consecrate you by His power, through His blood, that you are made pure and every bit holy—pure in mind, heart, and actions, pure right through.

God has given me the way of life, and I want to faithfully give it to you, as though this were the last day I had to live. Jesus is the best blessing, and you can take Him away with you this morning. God gave His Son to be *"the propitiation for [y]our sins, and not for [y]ours only but also for the whole world"* (1 John 2:2).

Jesus came to make us free from sin—free from disease and pain. When I see a person diseased and in pain, I have great compassion on him. When I lay my hands upon him, I know God intends for men to be so filled with Him that the power of sin has no effect on them. He intends for them to go forth, as I am doing, to help the needy, sick, and afflicted. But what is the main thing? To preach *"the kingdom of God and His righteousness"* (Matthew 6:33). Jesus came to do this. John also came preaching repentance. (See Mark 1:4.) The disciples began by preaching *"repentance toward God and faith toward our Lord Jesus Christ*" (Acts 20:21). I tell you, beloved, if you have really been changed by God, there is a repentance in your heart that you will never regret having there.

Through the revelation of the Word of God, we find that divine healing is solely for the glory of God. Moreover, salvation is to make you know that now you have to be inhabited by another, even God, and that now you have to walk with God "*in newness of life*" (Romans 6:4).

12

$\mathcal{D}o$ $\mathcal{Y}ou$ $\mathcal{W}ant$ to $\mathcal{B}e$ $\mathcal{M}ade$ $\mathcal{W}ell?$

I believe the Word of God is so powerful that it can transform any and every life. There is power in God's Word to make that which does not exist to appear. There is executive power in the words that proceed from His lips. The psalmist told us, *"He sent His Word and healed them"* (Psalms 107:20). Do you think the Word has diminished in its power? I tell you, it has not. God's Word can bring things to pass today as it did in the past.

The psalmist said, *"Before I was afflicted I went astray, but now I keep Your word"* (Psalm 119:67). And again, *"It is good for me that I have been afflicted, that I may learn Your statutes"* (verse 71). If our afflictions will bring us to the place where we see that we cannot *"live by bread alone, but by every word that proceeds from the mouth of God"* (Matthew 4:4), they will have served a blessed purpose. I want you to realize that there is a life of purity, a life made clean through the Word He has spoken, in which, through faith, you can glorify God with a body that is free from sickness, as well as with a spirit set free from the bondage of Satan.

Around the pool of Bethesda lay a great multitude of sick folk—blind, lame, paralyzed—waiting for the moving of the water. (See John 5:2–4.) Did Jesus heal all of them? No, He left many around that pool unhealed. Undoubtedly, many had their eyes on the pool and had no eyes for Jesus. There are many today who always have their confidence in things they can see. If they would only get their eyes on God instead of on natural things, how quickly they would be helped.

THE BREAD OF HEALING

The following question arises: Is salvation and healing for all? It is for all who will press right in and claim their portion. Do you remember the case of that Syro-Phoenician woman who wanted the demon cast out of her daughter? Jesus said to her, *"Let the children be filled first, for it is not good to take the children's bread and throw it to the little dogs"* (Mark 7:27). Note that healing and deliverance are here spoken of by the Master as *"the children's bread"*; therefore, if you are a child of God, you can surely press in for your portion.

The Syro-Phoenician woman purposed to get from the Lord what she was after, and she said, *"Yes, Lord, yet even the little dogs under the table eat from the children's crumbs"* (verse 28). Jesus was stirred as He saw the faith of this woman, and He told her, *"For this saying go your way; the demon has gone out of your daughter"* (verse 29).

Today many children of God are refusing their blood-purchased portion of health in Christ and throwing it away. Meanwhile, sinners are pressing through and picking it up from under the table and are finding the cure, not only for their bodies, but also for their spirits and souls. The Syro-Phoenician woman went home and found that the demon had indeed gone out of her daughter. Today there is bread—there is life and health—for every child of God through His powerful Word.

The Word can drive every disease away from your body. Healing is your portion in Christ, who Himself is our bread, our life, our health, our All in All. Though you may be deep in sin, you can come to Him in repentance, and He will forgive and cleanse and heal you. His words are spirit and life to those who will receive them. (See John 6:63.) There is a promise in the last verse of Joel that says, "*I will cleanse their blood that I have not cleansed*" (Joel 3:21 KJV). This as much as says that He will provide new life within. The life of Jesus Christ, God's Son, can so purify people's hearts and minds that they become entirely transformed—spirit, soul, and body.

The sick folk were around the pool of Bethesda, and one particular man had been there a long time. His infirmity was of thirty-eight years' standing. Now and again an opportunity to be healed would come as the angel stirred the waters, but he would be sick at heart as he saw another step in and be healed before him. Then one day Jesus was passing that way, and seeing him lying there in that sad condition, He asked, "*Do you want to be made well?*" (John 5:6). Jesus said it, and His words are from everlasting to everlasting. These are His words today to you, tried and tested one. You may say, like this poor sick man, "I have missed every opportunity up until now." Never mind that. "*Do you want to be made well?*"

IS IT THE LORD'S WILL?

I visited a woman who had been suffering for many years. She was all twisted up with rheumatism and had been in bed two years. I asked her, "What makes you lie here?" She said, "I've come to the conclusion that I have a thorn in the flesh." I said, "To what wonderful degree of righteousness have you attained that you must have a thorn in the flesh? Have you had such an abundance of divine revelations that there is a danger of your being exalted above measure?" (See 2 Corinthians 12:7–9.) She said, "I believe it is the Lord who is causing me to suffer." I said, "You believe it is the Lord's will for you to suffer, but you are trying to get out of it as quickly as you can. You have medicine bottles all over the place. Get out of your hiding place, and confess that you are a sinner. If you'll get rid of your self-righteousness, God will do something for you. Drop the idea that you are so holy that God has to afflict you. Sin is the cause of your sickness, not righteousness. Disease is not caused by righteousness, but by sin."

There is healing through the blood of Christ and deliverance for every captive. God never intended His children to live in misery because of some affliction that comes directly from the devil. A perfect atonement was made at Calvary. I believe that Jesus bore my sins, and I am free from them all. I am justified from all things if I dare to believe. (See Acts 13:39.) *"He Himself took our infirmities and bore our sicknesses"* (Matthew 8:17), and if I dare to believe, I can be healed.

See this helpless man at the pool. Jesus asked him, *"Do you want to be made well?"* (John 5:6). But there was a difficulty in the way. The man had one eye on the pool and one eye on Jesus. If you will look only to Christ and put both of your eyes on Him, you can be made every bit whole—spirit, soul, and body. It is the promise of the living God that those who believe are justified, made free, from all things. (See Acts 13:39.) And *"if the Son makes you free, you shall be free indeed"* (John 8:36).

You say, "Oh, if I could only believe!" Jesus understands. He knew that the helpless man had been in that condition for a long time. He is full of compassion. He knows about that kidney trouble; He knows about those corns; He knows about that neuralgia. There is nothing

He does not know. He wants only a chance to show Himself merciful and gracious to you, but He wants to encourage you to believe Him. If you can only believe, you can be saved and healed. Dare to believe that Jesus was wounded for your transgressions, was bruised for your iniquities, was chastised that you might have peace, and that by His stripes there is healing for you here and now. (See Isaiah 53:5.) You have failed because you have not believed Him. Cry out to Him even now, "*Lord, I believe; help my unbelief!*" (Mark 9:24).

I was in Long Beach, California, one day. I was with a friend, and we were passing by a hotel. He told me of a doctor there who had a diseased leg. He had been suffering from it for six years and could not get around. We went up to his room and found four doctors there. I said, "Well, doctor, I see you have plenty going on. I'll come again another day." I was passing by another time, and the Spirit said, "Go see him." Poor doctor! He surely was in poor shape. He said, "I have been like this for six years, and nobody can help me." I said, "You need almighty God." People are trying to patch up their lives, but they cannot do anything without God. I talked to him for a while about the Lord and then prayed for him. I cried, "Come out of him in the name of Jesus." The doctor cried, "It's all gone!"

Oh, if we only knew Jesus! One touch of His might meets the need of every crooked thing. The trouble is getting people to believe Him. The simplicity of this salvation is so wonderful. One touch of living faith in Him is all that is required for wholeness to be your portion.

I was in Long Beach about six weeks later, and the sick were coming for prayer. Among those filling up the aisle was the doctor. I said, "What is the trouble?" He said, "Diabetes, but it will be all right tonight. I know it will be all right." There is no such thing as the Lord's not meeting your need. There are no *ifs* or *mays*; His promises are all shalls. *"All things are possible to him who believes"* (Mark 9:23). Oh, the name of Jesus! There is power in that name to meet every human need.

At that meeting there was an old man helping his son to the altar. He said, "He has fits—many every day." Then there was a woman with cancer. Oh, what sin has done! We read that when God brought forth His people from Egypt, *"there was not one feeble person among their tribes"* (Psalm 105:37 KJV). No disease! All healed by the power of God! I believe that God wants a people like that today.

I prayed for the woman who had the cancer, and she said, "I know I'm free and that God has delivered me." Then they brought the boy with the fits, and I commanded the evil spirits to leave in the name of Jesus. Then I prayed for the doctor. At the next night's meeting the house was full. I called out, "Now, doctor, what about the diabetes?" He said, "It is gone." Then I said to the old man, "What about your son?" He said, "He hasn't had any fits since." We have a God who answers prayer.

SIN AND SICKNESS

Jesus meant this man at the pool to be a testimony forever. When he had both eyes on Jesus, He said to him, "Do the impossible thing. *'Rise, take up your bed and walk'* (John 5:8)." Jesus once called on a man with a withered hand to do the impossible—to stretch forth his hand. The man did the impossible thing. He stretched out his hand, and it was made completely whole. (See Matthew 12:10–13.)

In the same way, this helpless man began to rise, and he found the power of God moving within him. He wrapped up his bed and began to walk off. It was the Sabbath day, and there were some folks who, because they thought much more of a day than they did of the Lord, began to make a fuss. When the power of God is being manifested, a protest will always come from some hypocrites. Jesus knew all about what the man was going through and met him again. This time He said to him, "*See, you have been made well. Sin no more, lest a worse thing come upon you*" (John 5:14).

There is a close relationship between sin and sickness. How many know that their sicknesses are a direct result of sin? I hope that no one will come to be prayed for who is living in sin. But if you will obey God and repent of your sin and stop it, God will meet you, and neither your sickness nor your sin will remain. "*The prayer of faith will save the sick, and the Lord will raise him up. And if he has committed sins, he will be forgiven*" (James 5:15).

Faith is just the open door through which the Lord comes. Do not say, "I was saved by faith" or "I was healed by faith." Faith does not save and heal. God saves and heals through that open door. You believe, and the power of Christ comes. Salvation and healing are for the glory of God. I am here because God healed me when I was dying, and I have been around the world preaching this full redemption, doing all I can to bring glory to the wonderful name of the One who healed me.

"*Sin no more, lest a worse thing come upon you*" (John 5:14). The Lord told us in one place about an evil spirit going out of a man. The house that the evil spirit left got all swept and put in order, but it received no new occupant. That evil spirit, with seven other spirits more wicked than himself, went back to that unoccupied house, and "*the last state of that man* [was] *worse than the first*" (Matthew 12:45).

The Lord does not heal you to go to a baseball game or to a race-track. He heals you for His glory so that from that moment your life will glorify Him. But this man remained stationary. He did not magnify God. He did not seek to be filled with the Spirit. And his last state became "*worse than the first.*"

The Lord wants to so cleanse the motives and desires of our hearts that we will seek one thing only, and that is His glory. I went to a certain place one day and the Lord said, "This is for My glory." A young man had been sick for a long time. He had been confined to his bed in an utterly hopeless condition. He was fed with a spoon and was never dressed. The weather was damp, so I said to the people in the house, "I wish you would put the young man's clothes by the fire to air." At first they would not take any notice of my request, but because I was persistent, they at last got out his clothes. When they had been aired, I took them into his room.

The Lord said to me, "You will have nothing to do with this," and I just lay prostrate on the floor. The Lord showed me that He was going to shake the place with His glory. The very bed shook. I laid my hands on the young man in the name of Jesus, and the power fell in such a way that I fell with my face to the floor. In about a quarter of an hour, the young man got up and walked back and forth praising God. He dressed himself and then went out to the room where his father and mother were. He said, "God has healed me." Both the father and mother fell prostrate to the floor as the power of God surged through that room. There was a woman in that house who had been in an asylum for lunacy, and her condition was so bad that they were about to take her back. But the power of God healed her, too.

The power of God is just the same today as it was in the past. Men need to be taken back to the old paths, to the old-time faith, to believing God's Word and every "Thus says the Lord" in it. The Spirit of the Lord is moving in these days. God is coming forth. If you want to be in the rising tide, you must accept all God has said.

"Do you want to be made well?" (John 5:6). It is Jesus who asks this question. Give Him your answer. He will hear, and He will answer.

Smith Wigglesworth on
Spirit-Filled Living

13

A Face-to-Face Encounter with God

"Y our father has deceived me and changed my wages ten times, but God did not allow him to hurt me" (Genesis 31:7). To his father-in-law, Jacob said:

> Unless the God of my father...had been with me, surely now you would have sent me away empty-handed. God has seen my affliction and the labor of my hands.　　　　　(verse 42)

GOD'S WAY IS BEST

Jacob had been out in the bitter frost at night watching the flocks. He was a thrifty man, a hard worker, a planner, a supplanter. We see supplanters in our world today. They may experience a measure of blessing, but God is not first in their lives. We are not judging them, but there is a better way. It is better than our best. It is God's way. Scripture tells us: "There is a way that seems right to a man, but its end is the way of death" (Proverbs 16:25).

There is a way that God establishes. In our human planning, we may experience blessings of a kind, but we also undergo trials, hardships, and barrenness that God would have kept from us if we had followed His way. I realize through the anointing of the Holy Spirit that there is a freshness, a glow, a security in God where you can know that God is with you all the time. There is a place to reach where all that God has for us can flow through us to a needy world all the time: *"For as the heavens are higher than the earth, so are My ways higher than your ways, and My thoughts than your thoughts"* (Isaiah 55:9).

ALONE WITH GOD

Jacob was given time to think: *"Then Jacob was left alone; and a Man wrestled with him until the breaking of day."* Oh, to be left alone with God! In the context of the Scripture, we read that several things had preceded his being alone. His wives and his children had been sent ahead. His sheep, oxen, camels, and donkeys had gone ahead. He was alone.

Often, you will find that you are left alone. Whether you like it or not, you will be left alone like Jacob was left alone. His wives could not make atonement for him; his children could not make atonement for him; his money was useless to help him.

What made Jacob come to that place of loneliness, weakness, and knowledge of himself? He recalled the memory of the grace with which God had met him twenty-one years before, when he saw the ladder and the angels and heard the voice of God: *"Behold, I am with you and will keep you wherever you go, and will bring you back to this land; for I will not leave you until I have done what I have spoken to you"* (Genesis 28:15). He remembered God's mercy and grace.

He was returning to meet his brother Esau, who had become very rich. Esau had been blessed abundantly in the things of this world. He had authority and power to take all that Jacob had and to take vengeance upon him. Jacob knew this. He also knew that there was only one way of deliverance. What was it? Only God could keep Jacob safe. God had met him twenty-one years before when he had left home empty-handed. Now, he was returning with wives, children, and goods, but he was lean in soul and impoverished in spirit. Jacob said to himself, "If I do not get a blessing from God, I can never meet Esau," and he made up his mind he would not go on until he knew that he had favor with God. Jacob was left alone. Unless we get alone with God, we will surely perish. God intervenes when conflict exists. The way of revelation is plain. The Holy Spirit's plan is so clear that we have to say it was God after all.

Jacob was left alone. He knelt alone. The picture is so real to me. Alone! He began to think. He thought about the ladder and the angels. I think as he began to pray, his tongue stuck to the roof of his mouth. Jacob had to get rid of a lot of things. It had all been Jacob! As he got alone with God, he knew it. If you get alone with God, you will find it to be a place of revelation. Jacob was left alone, alone with God. We stay too long with our relations, our camels, and our sheep. Jacob was left alone. Hour after hour passed. He began to feel the presence of God, but he still had not received the desired blessing.

THE WAY TO VICTORY

If ever God is disappointed with you when you wait in His presence, it will be because you are not fervent. If you are not serious and intense, you disappoint God. If God is with you and you know it, be in earnest. Pray and believe: *"Hold fast the confidence and the rejoicing of the hope firm to the end*" (Hebrews 3:6). If you do not, you disappoint God.

Jacob was that way. God said, "You are not real enough; you are not hot enough; you are too ordinary; you are no good to Me unless you are filled with zeal—white hot!" The Angel of the Lord said, "*Let Me go, for the day breaks*" (Genesis 32:26). Jacob knew if God went without blessing him, he could not meet Esau. If you are left alone with God and you cannot get to a place of victory, it is a terrible time. You must never let go, whatever you are seeking—fresh revelation, light for your path, some particular need—never let go. Victory is ours if we are earnest enough. All must pass on; nothing less will please God. "*Let Me go, for the day breaks.*" He was wrestling with equal strength. Nothing is obtained that way.

You must always master that with which you are wrestling. If darkness covers you, if a fresh revelation is what you need, or if your mind needs to be relieved, always get the victory. God says you are not earnest enough. You say, "The Word does not say that." But it was in God's mind. In wrestling, the strength is in the neck, chest, and thigh; the thigh is the source of strength. So God touched his thigh. With that strength gone, defeat is sure. What did Jacob do? He hung on. God intends for people to be severed by the power of His power, so hold fast; He will never let go. If we let go, we will fall short.

Jacob said, "*I will not let You go unless You bless me!*" (Genesis 32:26). And God blessed him: "*Your name shall no longer be called Jacob, but Israel*" (verse 28). The change of Jacob to Israel was wonderful! Israel! Victory all the time! God is building all the time. God is sufficient all the time. Now Jacob has power over Esau, power over the world, power over the cattle. All is in subjection as he comes out of the great night of trial. The sun rises upon him. Oh, that God may take us on.

What happened after that? Read how God blessed and honored him. Esau meets him. There is no fighting now. What a blessed state of grace! They kiss each other: *"When a man's ways please the Lord, He makes even his enemies to be at peace with him"* (Proverbs 16:7).

"What about all these cattle, Jacob?"

"Oh, they are a present."

"I have plenty; I don't want your cattle. What a joy it is to see your face again!"

What a wonderful change! Who caused it? God.

HOLDING ON TO GOD

Could Jacob hold God? Can you hold God? Yes, you can. Sincerity can hold Him, dependence can hold Him, weakness can hold Him, for *"when [you are] weak, then [you are] strong"* (2 Corinthians 12:10). I'll tell you what cannot hold Him: self-righteousness cannot hold Him; pride cannot hold Him; assumption cannot hold Him; high-mindedness cannot hold Him—thinking you are something when you are nothing, puffed up in your imagination. You can hold Him in your prayer closet, in the prayer meeting, everywhere: *"If anyone hears My voice and opens the door, I will come in to him and dine with him, and he with Me"* (Revelation 3:20).

Can you hold Him? You may sometimes think that He has left you. Oh, no! He does not leave Jacob, Israel. What changed his name? The wrestling? What changed his name? The holding on, the clinging, the brokenness of spirit? If You do not help me, I am no good, no good for the world's need. I am no longer salt. Jacob obtained the blessing because of the favor of God and his yieldedness to God's will. God's Spirit was working in him to bring him to a place of helplessness. God worked to bring him to Bethel, the place of victory. Jacob remembered Bethel, and through all the trying circumstances, he had kept his vow. (See Genesis 28:20–22.)

When we make vows and keep them, God helps us. We must call upon God and give Him an account of the promise. *"And Jacob called the name of the place Peniel: 'For I have seen God face to face, and my life is preserved'"* (Genesis 32:30). How did he know? Do you know when God blesses you? Do you know when you have victory? Over twenty years later, the vision of the ladder and the angels remained with Jacob.

We must have a perfect knowledge of what God has for us. He knew that he had the favor of God, and that no man could hurt him. Let us in all our seeking see that we have the favor of God. Keep His commandments. Walk in the Spirit. Be tenderhearted and lovable. If we do these things, we will be appreciated by others, and our ministry will be a blessing to those who hear. God bless you. God bless you for Jesus' sake.

14

Filled with God

You may be filled with all the fullness of God.

(Ephesians 3:19)

Some people come with very small expectations concerning God's fullness, and a lot of people are satisfied with a thimbleful. You can just imagine God saying, "Oh, if they only knew how much they could take away!" Other people come with a larger container, and they go away satisfied. God is longing for us to have such a desire for more, a desire that only He can satisfy.

You women would have a good idea of what I mean from the illustration of a screaming child being passed from one person to another. The child is never satisfied until he gets to the arms of his mother. You will find that no peace, no help, no source of strength, no power, no life, nothing can satisfy the cry of the child of God but the Word of God. God has a special way of satisfying the cries of His children. He is waiting to open the windows of heaven until He has moved in the depths of our hearts so that everything unlike Himself has been destroyed. No one needs to go away empty. God wants you to be filled. My brother, my sister, God wants you today to be like a watered garden, filled with the fragrance of His own heavenly joy, until you know at last that you have touched the immense fullness of God. The Son of God came for no other purpose than to lift, to mold, and to remold, until *"we have the mind of Christ"* (1 Corinthians 2:16).

ASK LARGELY OF GOD

I know that dry ground can be flooded. (See Isaiah 44:3.) May God prevent me from ever wanting anything less than a flood. I will not settle for small things when I have such a big God. Through the blood of Christ's atonement, we may have riches and riches. We need the warming atmosphere of the Spirit's power to bring us closer and closer until nothing but God can satisfy. Then we may have some idea of what God has left after we have taken all that we can. It is like a sparrow taking a drink of the ocean and then looking around and saying, "What a vast ocean! What a lot more I could have taken if I only had room."

Sometimes you have things you can use, and you don't know it. You could be dying of thirst right in a river of plenty. There was once a boat in the mouth of the Amazon River. The people on board thought they were still in the ocean. They were dying of thirst, some of them nearly mad. They saw a ship and asked if they would give them some water. Someone on the ship replied, "Dip your bucket right over; you are in the mouth of the river." There are a number of people today in the middle of the great river of life, but they are dying of thirst because they do not dip down and take from the river.

Dear friend, you may have the Word, but you need an awakened spirit. The Word is not alive until it is moved upon by the Spirit of God, and in the right sense, it becomes Spirit and Life when it is touched by His hand alone.

Beloved, *"there is a river whose streams shall make glad the city of God, the holy place of the tabernacle of the Most High"* (Psalm 46:4). There is a stream of life that makes everything move. There is a touch of divine life and likeness through the Word of God that comes from nowhere else. We think of death as the absence of life, but there is a death-likeness in Christ, which is full of life.

There is no such thing as an end to God's beginnings. We must be in Christ; we must know Him. Life in Christ is not a touch; it is not a breath; it is the almighty God; it is a Person; it is the Holy One dwelling in the temple *"not made with hands"* (Hebrews 9:11). Oh, beloved, He touches, and it is done. He is the same God over all, *"rich to all who call upon Him"* (Romans 10:12). Pentecost is the last thing that God has to touch the earth with. If you do not receive the baptism of the Holy Spirit, you are living in a weak and impoverished condition, which is no good to yourself or anybody else. May God move us on to a place where there is no measure to this fullness that He wants to give us. God exalted Jesus and gave Him a name above every name. You notice that everything has been put under Him.

It has been about eight years since I was in Oakland, California, and since that time, I have seen thousands and thousands healed by the power of God. In the last five months of the year, we had over 7,000 people in Sweden saved by the power of God. The tide is rolling in. Let us see to it today that we get right into the tide, for it will hold us. God's heart of love is the center of all things. Get your eyes off yourself; lift them up high, and see the Lord, for in Him, there *"is everlasting strength"* (Isaiah 26:4).

If you went to see a doctor, the more you told him about yourself, the more he would know. But when you come to Doctor Jesus, He knows all from the beginning, and He never prescribes the wrong medicine. Jesus sends His healing power and brings His restoring grace, so there is nothing to fear. The only thing that is wrong is your wrong conception of His redemption.

TAKE AUTHORITY OVER SATAN

He was wounded that He might be able to identify with your weaknesses. (See Hebrews 4:15.) He took your flesh and laid it upon the cross that *"He might destroy him who had the power of death, that is, the devil, and release those who through fear of death were all their lifetime subject to bondage"* (Hebrews 2:14–15).

You will find that almost all the ailments that you experience come as a result of Satan, and they must be dealt with as satanic; they must be cast out. Do not listen to what Satan says to you, for the devil is a liar from the beginning. (See John 8:44.) If people would only listen to the truth of God, they would realize that every evil spirit is subject to them. They would find out that they are always in the place of triumph, and they would *"reign in life through the One, Jesus Christ"* (Romans 5:17).

Never live in a place other than where God has called you, and He has called you from on high to live with Him. God has designed that everything will be subject to man. Through Christ, He has given you authority over all the power of the Enemy. He has worked out your eternal redemption.

I was finishing a meeting one day in Switzerland. When the meeting ended and we had ministered to all the sick, we went out to see some people. Two boys came to us and said that there was a blind man present at the meeting that afternoon. He had heard all the words of the preacher and said he was surprised that he had not been prayed for. They went on to say that this blind man had heard so much that he would not leave until he could see. I said, "This is positively unique. God will do something today for that man."

We got to the place. The blind man said he had never seen. He was born blind, but because of the Word preached in the afternoon, he was not going home until he could see. If ever I have joy, it is when I have a lot of people who will not be satisfied until they get all that they have come for. With great joy, I anointed him and laid hands on his eyes. Immediately, God restored his vision. It was very strange how the man reacted. There were some electric lights. First he counted them; then he counted us. Oh, the ecstatic pleasure that this man experienced every moment because of his sight! It made us all feel like weeping and dancing and shouting. Then he pulled out his watch and said that for years he had been feeling the raised figures on the watch in order to tell the time. But now, he could look at it and tell us the time. Then, looking as if he had just awakened from some deep sleep, or some long, strange dream, he realized that he had never seen the faces of his father and mother. He went to the door and rushed out. That night, he was the first person to arrive for the meeting. All the people knew him as the blind man, and I had to give him a long time to talk about his new sight.

I wonder how much you want to take away today. You could not carry it if it were substance, but there is something about the grace, the power, and the blessings of God that can be carried, no matter how big they are. Oh, what a Savior. What a place we are in, by grace, that He may come in to commune with us. He is willing to say to every heart, *"Peace, be still"* (Mark 4:39), and to every weak body, *"Be strong"* (Deuteronomy 31:6).

Are you going halfway, or are you going all the way to the end? Do not be deceived by Satan, but believe God.

15

Above All You Can Ask or Think

To Him who is able to do exceedingly abundantly above all that
we ask or think...be glory.   (Ephesians 3:20–21)

Read Ephesians 3 carefully. This is a lovely chapter on Paul's mission to the Gentiles whom God has grafted in. Paul writes that previously it had not been revealed *"that the Gentiles should be fellow heirs, of the same body, and partakers of [God's] promise in Christ"* (verses 5–6). Paul had become a *"minister according to the gift of the grace of God given to [him] by the effective working of His power"* (verse 7). This power in Paul resulted in a very effective work. Although he was *"less than the least of all the saints"* (verse 8), he was given this grace of mystery and revelation. It came forth as a living reality of a living substance dwelling in him: *"to the intent that now the manifold wisdom of God might be made known by the church to the principalities and powers in the heavenly places"* (verse 10).

WISDOM

When we are completely humbled before God in a place where the Holy Spirit has full control, the wisdom of God is revealed to us. There alone, the vision comes to all His saints. We are now in the process of revelation. You must let the Holy Spirit perform His perfect function. I give myself to the leading of the manifold wisdom of God, "*in whom we have boldness and access with confidence through faith in Him*" (verse 12).

Boldness brings us into a place of access (see Hebrews 4:16), a place of confidence, laying hold, taking all off the table, and making it ours. In the human body, the Holy Spirit unfolds the mystery that we might know and have the revelation according to the will of God. The flesh is brought to a place of nonexistence, and the mighty power of God is shown to us. Paul responds by saying: "*I bow my knees to the Father*" (Ephesians 3:14).

PRAYER

Jude speaks of praying in the Holy Spirit. There is no natural line of thought here, not one point in particular upon which the mind can rest, but what is predicted from the throne of glory. Then the tongue and all the divine attributes are displayed above all, exceedingly above all, so that the glory of God may be revealed in the face of Jesus. God cannot display the greater glory except through those coequal in the glory, "*for we are His workmanship, created in Christ Jesus for good works*" (Ephesians 2:10). The Holy Spirit is the ideal and brings out the very essence of heaven through the human soul. We need the baptism of the Holy Spirit. Here we have the greatest liberty that can come to humanity; all the liberty of heaven is open to us. Praise the Father "*from whom the whole family in heaven and earth is named*" (Ephesians 3:15).

I love the thought that the veil is so thin that the tie between the family of God in heaven and the family of God on earth is closer than ever. Christ is with them, and they are with us. What loftiness, reverence, and holiness! This wedlock and fellowship in the Spirit is a wonderful thing. It results in an infinite mind of fulfillment and glory. *"Are they not all ministering spirits?"* (Hebrews 1:14). Who can help us more than those who have experienced the same trials as we? As the body is so fitly joined together by the effective working of His power, we are all one. Nothing separates us, but we look for the appearing of Jesus. He is there in glory, and they are with Him:

> *For the Lord Himself will descend from heaven with a shout, with the voice of an archangel, and with the trumpet of God. And the dead in Christ will rise first. Then we who are alive and remain shall be caught up together with them in the clouds to meet the Lord in the air. And thus we shall always be with the Lord.* (1 Thessalonians 4:16–17)

We can pray only as the Holy Spirit gives us the ability to express our thoughts. The Holy Spirit gives the highest principles through this prayer that the purposes of salvation are a continuous working and an increasing power all the time. The day that is coming will declare all things. We will be strengthened by the Spirit according to the riches of His glory.

GLORY

What is glory? All glory that ever comes is from Him. You have glory in the measure that you have the Son of glory in you. If you are filled with Jesus, you are filled with glory. When we have *"the spirit of wisdom and revelation in the knowledge of Him"* (Ephesians 1:17), there is nothing to hinder the Holy Spirit from having control of our whole beings.

"That Christ may dwell in your hearts through faith" (Ephesians 3:17). Faith is the production of all things. The Holy Spirit indwells and enlarges until the whole body is filled with Christ, and we are coming there in a very remarkable way. Did the Holy Spirit ever utter a prayer that no power could answer? In John 17:21, Jesus says: *"That they all may be one, as You, Father, are in Me, and I in You; that they also may be one in Us."* What works in us through being one with Him, through *"being rooted and grounded"* (Ephesians 3:17)? Perfect love, which has justice wrapped up in it. The day is coming when the saints will say "Amen" to the judgments of God. Justice will do it. All the wood, hay, and stubble must be destroyed (see 1 Corinthians 3:12), and we must be *"rooted and grounded"* in the Word.

I am a production of what God is forming, and I can arrest the gates of hell and laugh in the face of calamity and say, *"All things work together for good to those who love God"* (Romans 8:28). *"Rooted and grounded in love"* (Ephesians 3:17). Someone may leave me, but if I am grounded, it is for my good, and nothing can be against me but myself. We live for the glory of God. It is the Lord that establishes, strengthens, and upholds the weak, enabling them to withstand difficulties and to triumph in the day of battle. God is with you *"to do exceedingly abundantly above all that [you] ask or think."*

FAITH

Are we children of circumstances or children of faith? In our humanity, we may be troubled by the blowing of the wind. As it blows, it whispers fearfulness; but if you are *"rooted and grounded,"* you can stand the tests, and it is only then that you *"may be able to comprehend…what is the width and length and depth and height; to know the love of Christ which passes knowledge"* (Ephesians 3:18–19). It is an addition sum to meet every missionary's needs, to display God's power, enlarging what needs to be quickened.

What does Paul mean by the width of Christ's love? It is recognizing that God is sufficient in every circumstance. The length of His love indicates that God is in everything. God is in the depths and the heights! God is always lifting you, and the truth in that verse is enough for anyone in any circumstance to triumph. He *"is able to do exceedingly abundantly above all that we can ask or think,"* not according to the mind of Paul, but *"according to the power that works in us"* (verse 20). Simplicity of heart can broaden one's perspective, but this fullness is an ideal power of God in the human soul, enlarging every part. God is there instead of you to make you full, and you are full as your faith reaches out to be filled with all the fullness of God.

The power of the Lord was present to heal. His fullness of power flowed out of the disciples to others. In Acts 1, we see the power of God revealed as Jesus was lifted up to where He was before—into the presence of God. Jesus Christ showed the power of God in human flesh. The fullness of the Godhead was bodily manifested in Jesus. (See Colossians 2:9.) John says that *"in Him was life, and the life was the light of men"* (John 1:4). His substance revealed the fullness of God. How can it be fulfilled in me, you ask? The Scripture provides the answer: He is *"able to do exceedingly abundantly above all that we can ask or think."* It is filled there in the glory. But it's a tremendous thing. God will have to do something. Beloved, it is not according to your mind at all but according to the mind of God, according to the revelation of the Spirit. *"Above all that we can ask or think."* The blood has been poured out.

THE HOLY SPIRIT HAS BEEN GIVEN TO US

Truly, we are not worthy, but He is worthy. He will do more than we can even ask. How can it be possible? God puts it in your heart. He can do it. We hear much about rates of interest, but if you will faithfully follow God, He will add, enlarge, and lift you all the time, adding compound interest. Five percent? No! A thousand percent, a million percent! If you are willing, if holiness is the purpose of your heart, it will be done, for God is in His place. Will you be in the plan *"according to the power that works in* [you]*"* (Ephesians 3:20)? Whatever you are at any time, it will be by His effective power, lifting, controlling, and carrying you in constant rest and peace; it is *"according to the power that works in* [you]*."* Let all the people say: *"To Him be glory in the church by Christ Jesus to all generations, forever and ever. Amen"* (verse 21).

Smith Wigglesworth on the Anointing

16

"You Shall Receive Power"

You shall receive power when the Holy Spirit has come upon you" (Acts 1:8). The context of this passage is that the disciples had been asking whether the Lord would at that time restore the kingdom to Israel. (See verse 6.) Christ told them that it was not for them to know the times and seasons that the Father had put in His own power, but He promised them that when they received the Holy Spirit, they would receive power to witness for Him in all the world. (See verses 7–8.) To receive the Holy Spirit is to receive power with God and power with men.

There is a power that is of God, and there is a power that is of Satan. When the Holy Spirit fell in the early days of the Pentecostal outpouring we are experiencing, a number of Spiritists came to our meetings. They thought we had received something like they had, and they were coming to have a good time. They filled the two front rows of our mission. When the power of God fell, these imitators began their shaking and muttering under the power of the devil. The Spirit of the Lord came mightily on me, and I cried out, "Now, you devils, clear out of here!" And out they went. I followed them right out into the street, and then they turned around and cursed me. There was power from below, but it was no match for the power of the Holy Spirit, and they soon had to retreat.

POWER FROM ON HIGH

The Lord wants all saved people to receive *"power from on high"* (Luke 24:49)—power to witness, power to act, power to live, and power to show forth the divine manifestations of God within. The power of God will take you out of your own plans and put you into the plan of God. You will be unclothed and divested of what is purely of yourself and put into a divine order. The Lord will change you and put His mind where yours was, and thus enable you to have *"the mind of Christ"* (1 Corinthians 2:16). Instead of your working according to your own plan, it will be God working in you and through you to do His own good pleasure through the power of the Spirit within. (See Philippians 2:13.)

Someone has said that you are no good until you have your "I" knocked out. Christ must reign within, and life in the Holy Spirit means, at all times, the subjection of your own will to make way for the working out of the *"good and acceptable and perfect will of God"* within (Romans 12:2).

The Lord Jesus commanded that the disciples should tarry until they were *"endued with power from on high"* (Luke 24:49). In Acts 2, we read how the Spirit of God came. He comes in the same way today, and we don't know of the Holy Spirit coming in any other way.

Once, I was holding a meeting in London, and at the close of the meeting, a man came to me and said, "We are not allowed to hold meetings in this hall after eleven o'clock, and we would like you to come home with us. I am so hungry for God." His wife said that she, too, was hungry for God, and so I agreed to go with them. At about twelve-thirty, we arrived at their house. The man began stirring up the fire and said, "Now we will have a good supper." I said to them, "I did not come here for your warm fire, your supper, or your bed. I came here because I thought you were hungry to get more of God." We got down to pray, and at about three-thirty, the Lord baptized the wife, and she spoke in tongues as the Spirit gave utterance. (See Acts 2:4.) At about five o'clock, I spoke to the husband and asked how he was getting on. He replied, "God has broken my iron, stubborn will." He had not received the baptism, but God had worked a mighty work within him.

The following day, at his business, everyone could tell that a great change had come to him. Before, he had been a walking terror. The men who worked for him had looked upon him as a regular devil because of the way he had acted, but coming into contact with the power of God that night had completely changed him. Before this, he had made a religious profession, but he had never truly entered into the experience of the new birth until that night when the power of God surged so mightily through his home. A short while afterward, I went to this man's home, and his two sons ran to me and kissed me, saying, "We have a new father." Prior to this, these boys had often said to their mother, "Mother, we cannot stand it in the home any longer. We will have to leave." But the Lord changed the whole situation that night as we prayed together. On my second visit, the Lord baptized this man in the Holy Spirit. The Holy Spirit will reveal false positions, pull the mask off any *"refuge of lies"* (Isaiah 28:17), and clean up and remove all false conditions. When the Holy Spirit came in, that man's house and business, and he himself, were entirely changed.

THE HOLY SPIRIT COMES TO EMPOWER

When the Holy Spirit comes, He comes to empower you to be an effective witness. At one time, we were holding some special meetings, and I was out distributing handbills. I went into a shoemaker's store, and there was a man with a green shade and a cloth over his eyes. My heart looked up to the Lord, and I had the witness within that He was ready to change any condition. The man was crying, "Oh! Oh! *Oh!*" I asked, "What's the trouble?" He told me he was suffering from great inflammation and burning. I said, "I rebuke this condition in Jesus' name." Instantly, the Lord healed him. He took off the shade and the cloth, and said, "Look, it is all gone." I believe the Lord wants us to enter into real activity and dare to do for Him. *"You shall receive power when the Holy Spirit has come upon you"* (Acts 1:8).

At one time, a lady wrote and asked if I could go and help her. She said that she was blind, having two blood clots behind her eyes. When I reached the house, they brought the blind woman to me. We were together for some time, and then the power of God fell. Rushing to the window, she exclaimed, "I can see! Oh, I can see! The blood is gone; I can see." She then inquired about receiving the Holy Spirit and confessed that, for ten years, she had been fighting our position. She said, "I could not bear these tongues, but God has settled the whole thing today. I now want the baptism in the Holy Spirit." The Lord graciously baptized her in the Spirit.

THE HOLY SPIRIT WILL COME WHEN A PERSON IS CLEANSED

The Holy Spirit will come when a person is cleansed. There must be a purging of the old life. I never saw anyone baptized who was not clean within. I never saw a man baptized who smoked. We take it for granted that anyone who is seeking the fullness of the Spirit is free from such things as these. You cannot expect the third person of the Trinity to come into an unclean temple. There first must be a confession of all that is wrong, and a cleansing in the precious blood of Jesus Christ.

I remember being in a meeting where there was a man seeking the baptism, and he looked as though he was in trouble. He was very restless, and finally he said to me, "I will have to go." I said, "What's up?" He said, "God is unveiling things to me, and I feel so unworthy." I said, "Repent of everything that is wrong." He continued to tarry, and the Lord continued to search his heart. These times of waiting on God for the fullness of the Spirit are times when He searches the heart and tests the mind. (See Jeremiah 17:10.) Later, the man said to me, "I have a hard thing to do, the hardest thing I have ever had to do." I said to him, "Tell the Lord you will do it, and never mind the consequences." He agreed, and the next morning, he had to take a thirty-mile ride and go with a bag of gold to a certain party with whom he dealt. This man who was seeking the baptism had a hundred head of cattle, and he bought all his feed at a certain place. He always paid his accounts on a certain day, but one day he missed. He was always so punctual in paying his accounts that when the people of this firm later went over their books, they thought they must have made a mistake in not crediting the man with the money, and so they sent him a receipt. The man never intended not to pay the account, but if you delay doing a right thing, the devil will see to it that you never do it. But when the man was seeking the Lord that night, the Lord dealt with him on this point, and he had to go and straighten the thing out the next morning. He paid the account, and then the Lord baptized him in the Spirit. Those who carry the vessels of the Lord must be clean, must be holy. (See Isaiah 52:11.)

THE HOLY SPIRIT BRINGS A RICH REVELATION OF CHRIST

When the Holy Spirit comes, He always brings a rich revelation of Christ. Christ becomes so real to you that when, under the power of the Spirit, you begin to express your love and praise to Him, you find yourself speaking in another tongue. Oh, it is a wonderful thing! At one time, I belonged to a group who believed that they had received the baptism in the Spirit without the speaking in tongues. There are many people like that today; however, if you can go with them to a prayer meeting, you will find them asking the Lord again and again to baptize them in the Spirit. Why all this asking if they really have received the baptism? I have never heard people who have received the baptism in the Holy Spirit in accordance with the original pattern asking the Lord to give them the Holy Spirit. They know for certain that He has come.

I was once traveling from Belgium to England. When I landed in England, I received a request to stop at a place between Harwich and Colchester. The people there were delighted that God had sent me, and they told me of a special case they wanted me to pray for. They said, "We have a brother here who believes in the Lord, and he is paralyzed from his hips downward. He cannot stand on his legs, and he has been in this condition for twenty years." They took me to this man, and as I saw him there in his chair, I put the question to him, "What is the greatest desire in your heart?" He said, "Oh, if I could only receive the Holy Spirit!" I was somewhat surprised at this answer, and I laid my hands on his head and said, *"Receive the Holy Spirit"* (John 20:22). Instantly, the power of God fell on him, and he began breathing very heavily. He rolled off the chair, and there he lay like a bag of potatoes, utterly helpless. I like anything that God does. I like to watch God working. There he was, with his great, fat body, and his head was moving just as though it was on a swivel. Then, to our joy, he began speaking in tongues. I had my eyes on every bit of him, and as I saw the condition of his legs, I said, "Those legs can never carry that body." Then I looked up and said, "Lord, tell me what to do." The Holy Spirit carries out the will of Jesus Christ and the Father. If you want to know the mind of God, you must have the Holy Spirit to bring God's latest thought to you and to tell you what to do. The Lord said to me, "Command him in My name to walk." But I missed it, of course. I said to the people there, "Let's see if we can lift him up." But we could not lift him. It was as if he weighed a ton. I cried, "Oh, Lord, forgive me." I repented of doing the wrong thing, and then the Lord said to me again, "Command him to walk." I said to him, "Arise in the name of Jesus." His legs were immediately strengthened. Did he walk? He ran all around. A month after this, he walked ten miles and back. He has a Pentecostal ministry now. When the power of the Holy Spirit is present, things will happen.

There is still more for us all, praise the Lord. This is only the beginning. So far, we have only touched the fringe of things. There is so much more for us if we will only yield to God.

Do you want to receive the Spirit? *"If you then, being evil, know how to give good gifts to your children, how much more will your heavenly Father give the Holy Spirit to those who ask Him!"* (Luke 11:13). I am a father, and I want to give my boys the very best. We human fathers are only finite, but our heavenly Father is infinite. There is no limit to the power and blessing He has stored up for those who love Him. *"Be filled with the Spirit"* (Ephesians 5:18).

17

A New Plane of Existence

In days gone by, God's people have been persecuted and hunted. In Hebrews 11:38 we read of those *"of whom the world was not worthy. They wandered in deserts and mountains, in dens and caves of the earth."* We live in golden days in comparison—days of sunshine, prosperity, and hopefulness.

If those who have passed on before us wore such beautiful crowns in such times of strain and stress, our mouths should always be pouring forth tidal waves of blessing as the Holy Spirit has His way in these human bodies of ours and produces in us an eternal working: *"For our light affliction, which is but for the moment, is working for us a far more exceeding and eternal weight of glory"* (2 Corinthians 4:17).

The baptism of the Holy Spirit is a new plane of existence, a covering with the divine presence, a power burning in our very bones.

It is wonderful to be in the place where the truths of the Holy Spirit are so advanced. The day will soon dawn when the Daystar appears (see 2 Peter 1:19 KJV), and our one regret will be our lost opportunities of witnessing for God. May God make us a worthy people who embrace every opportunity.

THE POWER OF THE SPIRIT UPON PAUL

Paul had decided to sail past Ephesus, so that he would not have to spend time in Asia; for he was hurrying to be at Jerusalem, if possible, on the Day of Pentecost. (Acts 20:16)

Paul had seen Jesus by revelation on the road to Damascus, but he wanted to meet with those in Jerusalem who had seen Him as He walked the streets, as He healed the sick and raised the dead. Would you not like to talk with someone who had seen Him? Would you not like to ask, "What was His face like? What was His manner? How did He speak?" *"No man ever spoke like this Man!"* (John 7:46). Lots of people had seen Him around the table and on the roadways, and could testify to His wonderful works. No wonder Paul was hurrying to be at Jerusalem on the Day of Pentecost!

Paul remembered the days of Acts 9 when...

As he journeyed he came near Damascus, and suddenly a light shone around him from heaven. ...So the Lord said to [Ananias], "Arise and go to the street called Straight, and inquire at the house of Judas for one called Saul of Tarsus, for behold, he is praying." ...And Ananias went his way and entered the house; and laying his hands on him he said, "Brother Saul, the Lord Jesus, who appeared to you on the road as you came, has sent me that you may receive your sight and be filled with the

Holy Spirit." Immediately there fell from his eyes something like scales, and he received his sight at once; and he arose and was baptized. (Acts 9:3, 11, 17–18)

Paul was stirred as he remembered this mighty baptism in the Spirit, the victory that it had brought him into, and the power to preach the Gospel unlimited and unhindered that effectually worked in him. The mighty unction, or anointing, of the Holy Spirit remained upon him. We see this in the account of what happened at Troas:

When the disciples came together to break bread, Paul, ready to depart the next day, spoke to them and continued his message until midnight. There were many lamps in the upper room where they were gathered together. And in a window sat a certain young man named Eutychus, who was sinking into a deep sleep. He was overcome by sleep; and as Paul continued speaking, he fell down from the third story and was taken up dead. But Paul went down, fell on him, and embracing him said, "Do not trouble yourselves, for his life is in him." Now when he had come up, had broken bread and eaten, and talked a long while, even till daybreak, he departed. And they brought the young man in alive, and they were not a little comforted. (Acts 20:7–12)

Thus, with the unction of the Spirit upon him, Paul had gone down and fallen on the young man, embracing him in the power of the Spirit. Then Paul had returned and finished his message!

THE DAY OF PENTECOST

Now, in Acts 20:16, we find that the Day of Pentecost was near at hand. Again, what memories it had for Paul! We all look forward to observing Good Friday, when the cross of Calvary made an open door for all hearts to be saved; to commemorating Easter a few days later, when our Lord resurrected from the grave; and then to celebrating Whitsuntide or Pentecost and the wonderful descent of the Holy Spirit. When the Holy Spirit falls as He did at the beginning, He enlarges the hearts of all the people to live in the Spirit in such a way that there is new vision, new revelation, new equipping for service; new men are created. The baptism of the Holy Spirit means a new creation after the order of the Spirit.

INTERPRETATION OF TONGUES

For the Lord Himself descended by the power of the Spirit. "He shall not speak of Himself, and He will show you things to come." The baptism of the Holy Spirit is to fulfill in these bodies a new order—to everyone by a new power, to change from one state of grace to another—even by the Spirit of the Lord.

So Paul *"was hurrying to be at Jerusalem, if possible, on the Day of Pentecost"* (Acts 20:16). Understand, beloved, that many of the people at Jerusalem remembered the falling of the power as described in the second chapter of Acts.

There is a wonderful force of the anointing when all the people of God who are baptized with the Holy Spirit come together. What are religious conferences and conventions for? Their purpose is to meet the needs of those who are hungry and thirsty for God. Oh, this longing cry in the hearts of the people that can only be satisfied with more of God! On that memorable journey from Jerusalem to Damascus, Paul saw the risen Christ, and by the anointing of the Spirit, he became the greatest missionary the world has ever seen.

Oh, yes! There is something in unity, there is something in fellowship, there is something in being of one accord! Is the church today at such a place to receive? No! But God is in such a place to give. Who to? Only to thirsty, hungry souls. He has promised to fill *"the hungry with good things"* (Luke 1:53), and thus it will always be.

Now, what is the nature of a religious conference such as we are attending? It is a condition of not falling asleep, of not being lazy or apathetic; it is a condition of continual longing after God for a real outpouring of His Spirit. So Paul hurried to be at Jerusalem on the Day of Pentecost. Paul and the other believers expected wonderful things when they were once more in the Upper Room.

What was the plan as the disciples gathered together there? It was for preaching and telling the marvelous things that had happened.

> *Eye has not seen, nor ear heard, nor have entered into the heart of man the things which God has prepared for those who love Him. But God has revealed them to us through His Spirit.*
> (1 Corinthians 2:9–10)

The Holy Spirit is revealing and strengthening continually. This has been so from Pentecost on up until the present day.

An old man once stood up in a meeting and was referring to one person and then another who had passed on. He said, "All the good people are gone now." Another brother stood up and exclaimed, "Thank God, that's a lie!" Oh, yes! There are lots of people on the earth today who have seen Jesus.

Jesus, by the power of the Holy Spirit, is making me understand that we are only still in the beginnings of Pentecost. Get back to Pentecost. Remain in the anointing. Paul was hurrying to be at Jerusalem on the Day of Pentecost. Pentecost is the place where God can bestow such a measure of His love without limit, *"for God does not give the Spirit by measure"* (John 3:34).

A SEPARATING FORCE

The baptism of the Holy Spirit is not only the great essential power for victorious life and service, but it is also a separating force. Jesus said that a man's foes would often be those of his own household. (See Matthew 10:36.) It means separation, as sure as you live, if you follow the narrow way that leads to life. (Matt. 7:14.) It means persecution, but if you follow wholly, you will have no room for anything but Jesus. You will be bound in the Spirit, led on, on, on:

> And see, now I go bound in the spirit to Jerusalem, not knowing the things that will happen to me there, except that the Holy Spirit testifies in every city, saying that chains and tribulations await me. But none of these things move me; nor do I count my life dear to myself, so that I may finish my race with joy, and the ministry which I received from the Lord Jesus, to testify to the gospel of the grace of God. (Acts 20:22–24)

Another side of this is that the world narrows to you. There are thousands of believers who mean well, but who do not see the need of the baptism of the Holy Spirit. So, in the first place, the old group has no room for you, but in the second place, the Holy Spirit binds you. You have no room, only to go the way of the Spirit in conformity to the will of God; you are bound to go the narrow way.

I have never seen the Holy Spirit change His position: His way leads to simplicity in living, nonconformity to the world. You will not find God beginning in the Spirit and leading back to the flesh. Do you have no liberty to go back? If you want to turn back, ask yourself where you are going. What did Paul say? "I go bound in the Spirit to Jerusalem's bonds and afflictions." (See Acts 20:22–23.) He added,

None of these things move me; nor do I count my life dear to myself, so that I may finish my race with joy, and the ministry which I received from the Lord Jesus, to testify to the gospel of the grace of God. (Acts 20:24)

The way—the way of the cross—is separation from the flesh, nonconformity to the world, but with an ever deepening and enlarging in that abounding fullness of life that flows from the throne of God.

You must be in the right place spiritually in order to see "*Him who is invisible*" (Hebrews 11:27). Your mind must be operated by the Spirit, your desires under the control of the Spirit, and your plans directed and focused by the Spirit. (See Daniel 10.) Then, corruption is turned into comeliness. Then, your life in Christ becomes a wonderfully broad way, very broad, a perfection of complete orderliness. This is a state of being totally entrenched in the living God, bound in the Spirit! Can we take it in? There are depths we cannot fathom. I know it means bonds and afflictions. (See Acts 20:23 KJV) Shall I draw back? I cannot. Do you not see in Paul's willingness Jesus in a new form, Jesus again on the earth? This is the way we are bound to go. Paul called himself the "*bondservant*" of Jesus Christ. (See, for example, Romans 1:1.) But we are not obliged to be this! We could abandon our faith! Could I? Yes, I could! But I cannot! Separated bondservant, you cannot go back. It costs much to come, but it costs a thousand times more to retreat.

Oh, it's a costly thing to follow Jesus. Once having tasted the hidden manna, once having seen His face, it costs you your life to leave. (See Hebrews 6:4–6.) As Peter said, *"Lord, to whom shall we go? You have the words of eternal life"* (John 6:68).

INTERPRETATION OF TONGUES

The Lord is that Spirit, which has not only come in, but has embraced you and called you truly in the Spirit, that you might be a choice virgin betrothed to another, even Christ.

DEVOTED HEARTS

Shall we leave? No! Do you want to be unclothed? What a dreadful thing to be publicly exposed. (See Revelation 3:18.) What is it to be naked? To have a name for yourself! To be! And yet not to be! Lord, save us. Oh, for hearts that throb after the divine call. I love my Master. I do not want to be set free from serving Him. (See Exodus 21:5–6.)

This is no mediocre meeting; the Holy Spirit gently falls upon us. The Spirit of the living God yearns over us with tender compassion. God the Holy Spirit overshadows us. Some may say, "I want to get so near! I'll pay any price to come into this holy place!" Dear ones, you cannot take off your filthy garments. Christ unclothes your unrighteousness, and then He clothes you with the Holy Spirit! Oh, breathe every breath in the Holy Spirit. The old is taken away and the new is brought in, so that we never lose the fragrance of the divine presence, so that we fan and fan and fan until the Holy Spirit makes us living flames of fire carrying salvation everywhere, healing everywhere, the baptism of the Holy Spirit everywhere—on fire, bound forever, God thrilling the life.

INTERPRETATION OF TONGUES

It is the Lord Himself who has the choice of my heart, pruning to bring forth to His glory an eternal harvest gathered in forever.

There is something beautiful in the gift of tongues with interpretation, a joyfulness in experience—a sweet harmony establishing, fortifying, and making our hearts strong in Himself. The day is not far distant when we may have to stand very firm in what God is taking us on to. War, pestilence, famine—the order has not been altered since the world began. These are trying times for the believer. The world wants less of God and there is a great deal of trial of faith. Are we going to be found faithful? Two things will help you: faith and the baptism of the Holy Spirit. These will establish you against attacks or evil winds from any source.

We ought to be so established that we are ready and willing to be tried when the day comes, no matter which side the Spirit presses. There is always the thought that Jesus may come before that day, so that one is as likely as the other. God will strengthen your heart in the trial, in the evil day. He will never leave His own. Every man burned at the stake for the faith has been a seed, a light, a torch, bringing in a new order. Let us keep the vision clear—pure in heart, upward, onward, heavenward—*"until the day breaks and the shadows flee away"* (Song of Solomon 2:17).

Jesus is the loveliest on earth. The Holy Spirit clothes Him. He met the need of all. You belong to the *"church of the firstborn"* (Hebrews 12:23), the establishment of that wonderful place in the glory. Will you promise God that nothing will come between you and the throne—the heart of God and the mind of the Spirit? God has a choice for everyone *"who swears to his own hurt and does not change"* (Psalm 15:4)—a pressing right in.

Is my Jesus not beautiful? Could anything cloud that brow? He has the joy of redemption for us. We go from victory to victory. Your faces are a picture of what they will be in glory. Let us be zealous, setting to our seals that God is true, until that day when we will abide with Him forever. *"Set your house in order"* (2 Kings 20:1); you must go God's way—follow Him. The building is going up. The top stone must be put on. Grace, grace be unto it.

18

Immersed in the Holy Spirit

The baptism of the Holy Spirit is a great beginning. I think the best word we can say is, *"Lord, what do You want me to do?"* (Acts 9:6). The greatest difficulty with us today is to be held in the place where it will be God only. It is so easy to get our own minds to work. The working of the Holy Spirit is so different. I believe there is a mind of Christ (see 1 Corinthians 2:16), and we may be so immersed in the Spirit that we are asking all day, *"What do You want me to do?"*

This has been a day in the Holy Spirit. The last three months have been the greatest days of my life. I used to think that if I could see certain things happen, I would be satisfied; but I have seen greater things than I ever expected to see, and I am hungrier to see greater things still. The great thing about conferences is that we may get so immersed in God that we may see signs and wonders in the name of the Lord Jesus. This immersion in God is a place where death to self has taken place, and "we" are no longer, for God has taken us.

(See Hebrews 11:5.) If God has taken hold of us, we will be changed by His power and might. You can depend on it, the Ethiopian will be changed. (See Jeremiah 13:23.) I find that God has a plan to turn *"the world upside down"* (Acts 17:6), when we have died to self.

When I have been at my wits' end and have seen God open the door, I have felt as if I would never doubt God again. Then I have been taken to another place that was worse still. There is no place for us, and yet there is a place where God is, where the Holy Spirit is showing forth and displaying His graces, a place where we will never come out, where we are always immersed in the Spirit, the glory of God being seen upon us. It is wonderful! There is a power behind the scenes that moves things. God can work in such a marvelous way.

I believe we have yet to learn what it would be like with a Pentecostal church in England that truly understood the work of intercession. I believe God the Holy Spirit wants to teach us that it is not only the people on the platform who can move things by prayer, but that you people—the Lord can also move things through you. We have to learn the power of the breath of the Holy Spirit. If I am filled with the Holy Spirit, He will formulate the word that will come into my heart. The sound of my voice is made only by the breath that goes through it.

When I was in a little room at Bern, Switzerland, waiting for my passport, I found a lot of people, but I couldn't speak to them. So I got hold of three men and pulled them to me. They stared, but I got them on their knees. Then we prayed, and the revival began. I couldn't talk to them, but I could show them the way to talk to Someone else.

God will move upon the people to make them see the glory of God just as it was when Jesus walked in this world; and I believe the Holy Spirit will do special wonders and miracles in these last days.

I was taken to see a young woman who was very ill. The young man who showed me the way said, "I am afraid we will not be able to do much here because of her mother, and the doctors are coming." I said, "This is what God has brought me here for," and when I prayed, the young woman was instantly healed by the power of God. God the Holy Spirit says in our hearts today that it is only He who can do it. After the young woman's healing, a crowd gathered, and I ministered to the sick among them for two hours.

The secret for the future is living and moving in the power of the Holy Spirit. One thing I rejoice in is that there does not need to be an hour or a moment when I do not know that the Holy Spirit is upon me. Oh, this glorious life in God is beyond expression; it is God manifest in the flesh. Oh, this glorious anointing of the Holy Spirit—that we move by the Spirit. He should be our continual life. The Holy Spirit has the latest thoughts of anything that God wants to give. Glory to God for the Holy Spirit! We must see to it that we live in the place where we say, *"What do You want me to do?"* (Acts 9:6), and that we are in the place where He can work in us *"to will and to do for His good pleasure"* (Philippians 2:13).

Smith Wigglesworth on
Spiritual Gifts

19

Concerning Spiritual Gifts

God wants us to enter into the rest of faith. He desires us to have all confidence in Him. He purposes that His Word will be established in our hearts; and, as we believe His Word, we will see that *"all things are possible"* (Matthew 19:26).

In 1 Corinthians 12:1 we read, *"Now concerning spiritual gifts, brethren, I do not want you to be ignorant."* There is a great weakness in the church of Christ because of an awful ignorance concerning the Spirit of God and the gifts He has come to bring. God wants us to be powerful in every way because of the revelation of the knowledge of His will concerning the power and manifestation of His Spirit. He desires us to be continually hungry to receive more and more of His Spirit.

In the past, I have organized many conferences, and I have found that it is better to have a man on my platform who has not received the baptism but who is hungry for all that God has for him, than a man who has received the baptism and is satisfied and has settled down and become stationary and stagnant. But of course I would prefer a man who is baptized with the Holy Spirit and is still hungry for more of God. A man who is not hungry to receive more of God is out of order in any Christian conference.

THE IMPORTANCE OF BEING FILLED

It is impossible to overestimate the importance of being filled with the Spirit. It is impossible for us to meet the conditions of the day, to *"walk in the light as He is in the light"* (1 John 1:7), to subdue kingdoms and work righteousness and bind the power of Satan, unless we are filled with the Holy Spirit.

We read that, in the early church, *"they continued steadfastly in the apostles' doctrine and fellowship, in the breaking of bread, and in prayers"* (Acts 2:42). It is important for us also to continue steadfastly in these same things.

For some years I was associated with the Plymouth Brethren. They are very strong on the Word and are sound on water baptism. They do not neglect the communion service; rather, they have it on the morning of every Lord's Day, as the early church did. These people seem to have the wood and the kindling, but not the match. If they had the fire, then they would be all ablaze.

Because they lack the fire of the Holy Spirit, there is no life in their meetings. One young man who attended their meetings received the baptism with the speaking in other tongues as the Spirit gave utterance. (See Acts 2:4.) The brethren were very upset about this, and they came to the young man's father and said to him, "You must take your son aside and tell him to cease." They did not want any disturbance. The father told the son, "My boy, I have been attending this church for twenty years and have never seen anything of this kind. We are established in the truth and do not want anything new. We won't have it." The son replied, "If that is God's plan, I will obey, but somehow or other I don't think it is." As they were going home, the horse stood still; the wheels of their carriage were in deep ruts. The father pulled at the reins, but the horse did not move. He asked, "What do you think is up?" The son answered, "It has gotten established." God save us from becoming stationary.

God wants us to understand spiritual gifts and to *"earnestly desire the best gifts"* (1 Corinthians 12:31). He also wants us to enter into the *"more excellent way"* (verse 31) of the fruit of the Spirit. We must implore God for these gifts. It is a serious thing to have the baptism and yet be stationary. To live two days in succession on the same spiritual plane is a tragedy. We must be willing to deny ourselves everything to receive the revelation of God's truth and to receive the fullness of the Spirit. Only that will satisfy God, and nothing less must satisfy us.

A young Russian received the Holy Spirit and was mightily clothed with power from on high. The secret of his power was a continuous waiting upon God. As the Holy Spirit filled him, it seemed as though every breath became a prayer, and so his entire ministry was continually increasing.

I knew a man who was full of the Holy Spirit and would only preach when he knew that he was mightily anointed by the power of God. He was once asked to preach at a Methodist church. He was staying at the minister's house and he said, "You go on to church and I will follow." The place was packed with people, but this man did not show up. The Methodist minister, becoming anxious, sent his little girl to inquire why he did not come. As she came to the bedroom door, she heard him crying out three times, "I will not go." She went back and reported that she had heard the man say three times that he would not go. The minister was troubled about it, but almost immediately afterward the man came in. As he preached that night, the power of God was tremendously manifested. The preacher later asked him, "Why did you tell my daughter that you were not coming?" He answered, "I know when I am filled. I am an ordinary man, and I told the Lord that I did not dare to go and would not go until He gave me a fresh filling of the Spirit. The moment the glory filled me and overflowed, I came to the meeting."

Yes, there is a power, a blessing, an assurance, a rest in the presence of the Holy Spirit. You can feel His presence and know that He is with you. You do not need to spend an hour without this inner knowledge of His holy presence. With His power upon you, there can be no failure. You are above par all the time.

"You know that you were Gentiles, carried away to these dumb idols, however you were led" (1 Corinthians 12:2). This is the age of the Gentiles. When the Jews refused the blessings of God, He scattered them, and He has grafted the Gentiles into the olive tree where many of the Jews were broken off. (See Romans 11:17–25.) There has never been a time when God has been so favorable to a people who were not a people. (See 1 Peter 2:9–10.) He has brought in the Gentiles to carry out His purpose of preaching the Gospel to all nations and receiving the power of the Holy Spirit to accomplish this task. It is because of the mercy of God that He has turned to the Gentiles and made us partakers of all the blessings that belong to the Jews. Here, under this canopy of glory, because we believe, we get all the blessings of faithful Abraham.

GUARD AGAINST ERROR

Therefore I make known to you that no one speaking by the Spirit of God calls Jesus accursed, and no one can say that Jesus is Lord except by the Holy Spirit.   (1 Corinthians 12:3)

Many evil, deceiving spirits have been sent forth in these last days who endeavor to rob Jesus of His lordship and of His rightful place. Many people are opening the doors to these latest devils, such as New Theology and New Thought and Christian Science. These evil cults deny the fundamental truths of God's Word. They all deny eternal punishment and the deity of Jesus Christ. You will never see the baptism of the Holy Spirit come upon a man who accepts these errors. Nor will you see anyone receive the baptism who puts Mary in the place of the Holy Spirit. No one can know he is saved by works. If you ever speak to someone who believes this, you will know that he is not definite on the matter of the new birth. He cannot be. And there is another thing: you will never find a Jehovah's Witness baptized in the Holy Spirit. The same is true for a member of any other cult who does not believe that the Lord Jesus Christ is preeminent.

The all-important thing is to make Jesus Lord of your life. Men can become lopsided by emphasizing the truth of divine healing. Men can get into error by preaching on water baptism all the time. But we never go wrong in exalting the Lord Jesus Christ, in giving Him the preeminent place and glorifying Him as both Lord and Christ, yes, as "very God of very God." As we are filled with the Holy Spirit, our one desire is to glorify Him. We need to be filled with the Spirit to get the full revelation of the Lord Jesus Christ.

God's command is for us to *"be filled with the Spirit"* (Ephesians 5:18). We are no good if we only have a full cup. We need to have an overflowing cup all the time. It is a tragedy not to live in the fullness of overflowing. See that you never live below the overflowing tide.

USE THE GIFT PROPERLY

"There are diversities of gifts, but the same Spirit" (1 Corinthians 12:4). Every manifestation of the Spirit is given *"for the profit of all"* (verse 7). When the Holy Spirit is moving in an assembly of believers and His gifts are in operation, everyone will profit.

I have seen some people who have been terribly off track. They believe in gifts—prophecy, in particular—and they use these gifts apart from the power of the Holy Spirit. We must look to the Holy Spirit to show us how to use the gifts, what they are for, and when to use them, so that we may never use them without the power of the Holy Spirit. I do not know of anything that is so awful today as people using a gift without the power. Never do it. God save us from doing it.

While a man who is filled with the Holy Spirit may not be conscious of having any gift of the Spirit, the gifts can be made manifest through him. I have gone to many places to minister, and I have found that, under the unction, or anointing, of the Holy Spirit, many wonderful things have happened in the midst of the assembly when the glory of the Lord was upon the people. Any man who is filled with God and filled with His Spirit might at any moment have any of the nine gifts listed in 1 Corinthians 12 made manifest through him, without knowing that he has a gift.

Sometimes I have wondered whether it is better to be always full of the Holy Spirit and to see signs and wonders and miracles without any consciousness of possessing a gift or whether it is better to know one has a gift. If you have received the gifts of the Spirit and they have been blessed, you should never under any circumstances use them without the power of God upon you pressing the gift through. Some have used the prophetic gift without the holy touch, and they have come into the realm of the natural. It has brought ruin, caused dissatisfaction, broken hearts, and upset assemblies. Do not seek the gifts unless you have purposed to abide in the Holy Spirit. They should be manifested only in the power of the Holy Spirit.

USE THE GIFTS WITH WISDOM

The Lord will allow you to be very drunk in the Spirit in His presence, but sober among people. I like to see people so filled with the Spirit that they are drunk in the Spirit like the 120 disciples were on the Day of Pentecost, but I don't like to see people drunk in the Spirit in the wrong place. That is what troubles us: somebody being drunk in the Spirit in a place of worship where a lot of people come in who know nothing about the Word. If you allow yourself to be drunk there, you send people away; they look at you instead of seeing God. They condemn the whole thing because you have not been sober at the right time.

Paul wrote, "For if we are beside ourselves, it is for God; or if we are of sound mind, it is for you" (2 Corinthians 5:13). You can be beside yourself. You can go a bit further than being drunk; you can dance, if you will do it at the right time. So many things are commendable when all the people are in the Spirit. Many things are very foolish if the people around you are not in the Spirit. We must be careful not to have a good time in the Lord at the expense of somebody else. When you have a good time, you must see that the spiritual conditions in the place lend themselves to it and that the people are falling in line with you. Then you will always find it a blessing.

While it is right to earnestly desire the best gifts, you must recognize that the all-important thing is to be filled with the power of the Holy Spirit Himself. You will never have trouble with people who are filled with the power of the Holy Spirit, but you will have a lot of trouble with people who have the gifts but no power. The Lord does not want us to *"come short"* in any gift (1 Corinthians 1:7). But at the same time, He wants us to be so filled with the Holy Spirit that it will be the Holy Spirit manifesting Himself through the gifts. Where the glory of God alone is desired, you can expect that every gift that is needed will be made manifest. To glorify God is better than to idolize gifts. We prefer the Spirit of God to any gift; but we can see the manifestation of the Trinity in the gifts: different gifts but the same Spirit, different administrations but the same Lord, diversities of operation but the same God working all in all. (See 1 Corinthians 12:4–6.) Can you conceive of what it will mean for our triune God to be manifesting Himself in His fullness in our assemblies?

Imagine a large locomotive boiler that is being filled with steam. You can see the engine letting off some of the steam as it remains stationary. It looks as though the whole thing might burst. You can see believers who are like that. They start to scream, but that does not edify anyone. However, when the locomotive moves on, it serves the purpose for which it was built and pulls along many cars with goods in them. It is the same way with believers when they are operating in the gifts of the Spirit properly.

INWARD POWER MANIFESTED OUTWARDLY

It is wonderful to be filled with the power of the Holy Spirit and for Him to serve His own purposes through us. Through our lips, divine utterances flow, our hearts rejoice, and our tongues are glad. It is an inward power that is manifested in outward expression. Jesus Christ is glorified. As your faith in Him is quickened, from within you there *"will flow rivers of living water"* (John 7:38). The Holy Spirit will pour through you like a great river of life, and thousands will be blessed because you are a yielded channel through whom the Spirit may flow.

20

How to Receive a Spiritual Gift

The gift of the Holy Spirit, which He breathes into you, will make you wonderfully alive. It will almost seem as though you had never been born before. The jealousy God has over us, the interest He has in us, the purpose He has for us, the grandeur of His glory are so marvelous. God has called us into this place to receive gifts.

Now I want to tell you how to receive a gift. I will illustrate this by explaining the nature of a gift and telling you what happened to me when I received the gift of tongues.

The difference between speaking in tongues as a gift and speaking in tongues by receiving the Spirit is this: everybody who is baptized speaks as the Spirit gives utterance. The tongues that are manifested when someone receives the baptism are an evidence of the baptism. However, this is not the gift of tongues. The gift is a special manifestation in a person's life that he knows, and he can speak in tongues as long as he wants to. Nevertheless, a person should never speak longer than the Spirit gives the anointing; he should never go beyond the Spirit's leading. Like someone giving a prophecy, he should never go beyond the spiritual anointing.

The trouble is this: after we have been blessed with tongues, our human nature often steps in. Everything that is not the rising tide of the Spirit is either law or letter. (See Romans 7:6–7.) What does this mean? When you are following the law, it means that you have fallen into your human nature. When you are following the letter, it means that you are depending upon the Word without the power. These two things will work against you instead of working for you.

The letter and the law bring harshness; the Spirit brings joy and happiness. One is perfect harmony; the other produces strife. One is the higher tide of the Spirit; the other is earthly. One gets into the bliss of the presence of heaven; the other never rises from earthly associations.

Claim your right; claim your position. The person who asks for a gift twice will never get it under any circumstances. I am not moved by what you think about it. I believe this is sovereign from God's altar. You never get a gift if you ask for it twice. But God will have mercy upon you if you stop asking and believe.

There is not a higher order that God puts in motion with a person who believes than this: *"Ask, and you will receive"* (John 16:24). If you dare to ask for any gift, if you really believe that it is a necessary gift, if you dare to ask and will not move from it but begin to act in it, you will find that the gift is there.

If you want to be in the will of God, you will have to be stubborn. What do I mean by this? I mean that you will have to be unchangeable. Do you think that if you get a gift, you will feel it? It is nothing like that. If you ask for a gift, do not expect that there will be a feeling with it. There is something better; there is a fact with it, and the fact will bring the feeling after the manifestation. People want feelings for gifts. There is no such thing. You will make the biggest mistake if you dare to continue praying about anything until you feel like doing something. As sure as can be, you have lost your faith. You have to believe that after you receive, you have the power, and that you begin to act in the power.

The morning after I received the gift of tongues, I went out of the house with a box of tools on my back; I was going down the street to do some work. The power of God lit me up and I broke out in tongues—loudly. My, they were loud! The street was filled with people, and there were some gardeners trimming some hedges and cutting the grass. When they heard me, they stuck their heads over the hedges, looking as if they had swan necks.

"Whatever is up? Why, it is the plumber."

I said, "Lord, I am not responsible for this, and I won't go from this place until I have the interpretation."

God knows that I wouldn't have moved from that place. And out came the interpretation:

Over the hills and far away before the brink of day, the Lord your God will send you forth and prosper all your way.

This is the point: the gift was there. I did not pray for it. I did not say, "Lord, give me the interpretation." I said, "If you don't give it to me, I won't move." By this I meant that I was determined to have the gift.

It has been surprising, but at every place where I am, the Spirit of the Lord moves upon me.

I want to say something about the gift of interpretation because it is so sublime, it is so divine, it is such a union with the Christ. It is a pleasing place with the Christ. It is not the Holy Spirit who is using it so much, but it is the Christ who is to be glorified in that act, for the Trinity moves absolutely collectively in the body.

As soon as that incident had taken place, wherever I went, when anybody spoke in tongues, I did not say, "Lord, give me the interpretation." That would have been wrong. I lived in a fact. Now, what is a fact? A fact is what produces. Fact produces; fact has it. Faith is a fact. Faith moves fear and faction. Faith is audacity. Faith is a personality. Faith is the living Christ manifested in the believer.

Now, what is interpretation? Interpretation moves and brings forth the words of God without the person thinking about it. If you get words before you have received from God, that is not interpretation. The person who interprets does not have the words. The gift breathes forth, and the person speaks, never stopping until he is through. He does not know what he is going to say until the words are out. He does not form them; he does not plan them. Interpretation is a divine flood, just as tongues are a flood. So it requires continual faith to produce this thing.

A divine gift has divine comprehension. It is also full of prophetic utterances. There is no such thing as an end to the divine vocabulary.

What is faith? Is it a pledge? It is more than that. Is it a present? It is more than that. It is relationship. Now, is there something better than relationship? Yes. What is it? Sonship is relationship, but heirship is closer still; and faith is *"God...manifested in the flesh"* (1 Timothy 3:16).

"What was Jesus?" you ask.

Jesus was the glory manifested in human incarnation.

"Was He anything else?"

Yes. Jesus was the fullness of the *"express image"* of the Father (Hebrews 1:3). Is that fullness ours? Yes. Who are the chosen ones? They are those who ask and believe and see it done. God will make you chosen if you believe it.

Let us repent of everything that is hindering us; let us give place to God. Let us lose ourselves in Him. Let us have no self-righteousness, but let us have brokenness, humbleness, submission. Oh, may there be such broken-heartedness in us today! May we be dead indeed and alive indeed with refreshing from the presence of the Most High God!

Some of you have been saying, "Oh, I wish I could know how to get a gift." Some of you have felt the striving of the Holy Spirit within you. Oh, beloved, rise to the occasion this day. Believe God. Ask God for gifts, and it may come to pass in your life. But do not ask unless you know it is the desire of your heart. God grant to us gifts and graces!

21

Love and the Gifts

Thank God for the Word that comes to us afresh! Early this morning I was thinking and wondering if the Lord would speak through me, and I was strongly impressed that I should read to you 1 Corinthians 13.

I am so thankful to God that He has dovetailed this thirteenth chapter of 1 Corinthians between the twelfth and the fourteenth. The twelfth chapter deals expressly with the gifts of the Spirit, and the fourteenth chapter is on the lines of the manifestations and the gifts of the Spirit; the thirteenth chapter functions similarly to the governor balls that control a steam engine. If you ever see this type of engine working, you will find that right over the main valve that lets in the steam, there are two little balls that go around. Often they go as fast as they can, though sometimes they go slowly. They open and shut the valve that sends the steam to the pistons. These are constructed so that the engine does not get out of control.

I find that God, the Holy Spirit, in His remarkable wisdom, has placed the thirteenth chapter right between these wonderful chapters on the gifts that we love to dwell upon so much. How wonderful, how magnificent they are! God has given them to us so that we may be useful, not ornamental, and prove in every case and under every circumstance that we might be available at the right time with these gifts. They are enduement for power; they are expressive of His love; they are for the edification and comfort of so many weary souls.

We find that God brings these gifts in perfect order so that the church may receive blessings. Yet how many people, how many of us, have failed to come to the summit of perfection because the governor balls were not working well, because we were more taken up with the gift than the power that moved the gift, because we were more frequently delighted in the gift than the Giver of the gift! Then the gift became fruitless and helpless, and we were sorry. Sometimes it brought on rebuke, and sometimes we suffered, suffered more or suffered less.

INTERPRETATION OF TONGUES

The love that constrains, the grace that adorns, the power that sustains, the gift that remains may be in excellence, when He is the Governor, the Controller, the Worker.

I do thank God for tongues and interpretation, because they introduce new vision; they open the larger avenue. Let it please You today, Lord, to show us how to work and how to walk and not stumble.

THE GIFTS

Now, beloved, the topic of love and the gifts is a very large one. However, I will do all I can, by the grace of God, so that I may say things that will live after I have gone away. For it is very necessary that we receive the Holy Spirit in the first place; after receiving the Holy Spirit, we must earnestly desire the gifts. Then, after receiving the gifts, we must never forget that the gift is entrusted to us for bringing the blessings of God to the people.

For instance, divine healing is a gift for ministering to the needs of the people. The gift of wisdom is a word in season at the moment of need, to show you just what to do. The gift of knowledge, or the word of knowledge, is to inspire you because of the consecutiveness of the Word of God, to bring you life and joy. This is what God intends.

Then there is the gift of discernment. We are not to discern one another, but to discern evil powers and deal with them and command them back to the pit from which they came. Regarding the gift of miracles, God intends for us to come to the place where we will see miracles worked. God also wants us to understand that tongues are profitable only when they exalt and glorify the Lord. And oh, that we might really know what it means when interpretation is given! It is not merely to have beautiful sensations and think that is interpretation, but it is such that the man who has it does not know what is coming, for if he did, it would not be interpretation. Interpretation is not knowing what you are going to say, but it is being in the place where you say exactly what God says. So when I have to interpret a message, I purposely keep my mind from anything that would hinder, and I sometimes say "Praise the Lord" and "Hallelujah" so that everything will be a word through the Spirit, and not my word, but the word of the Lord!

Now I understand that we can have these divine gifts so perfectly balanced by divine love that they will be a blessing all the time.

However, there is sometimes such a desire in the flesh to do something attention-getting. How the people listen and long for divine prophecy, just as interpretation comes forth. How it thrills! There is nothing wrong with it; it is beautiful. We thank God for the office and the purpose that has caused it to come, but let us be careful to finish when we are through and not continue on our own. That is how prophecy is spoiled. If you continue on your own, at the end of the anointing, you are using false fire; at the end of the message, you will try to continue. Don't fail, beloved, because the people know the difference. They know what is full of life, what is the real thing.

Then again, it is the same with a person praying. We love people to pray in the Holy Spirit; how we love to hear them pray even the first sentences because the fire is there. However, what spoils the most holy person in prayer is when, after the spirit of prayer has gone forth, he continues on and people say, "I wish he would stop," and the church becomes silent. They say, "I wish that brother would stop. How beautifully he began; now he is dry!" But he doesn't stop.

A preacher was once having a wonderful time, and the people enjoyed it, but when he was through, he continued. A man came and said to someone at the door, "Has he finished?" "Yes," said the man, "long since, but he won't stop!" May God save us from that. People know when you are praying in the Spirit. Why should you take time and spoil everything because the natural side has come into it? God never intended that. God has a supernatural side; that is the true side, and how beautiful it is! People sometimes know better than we do, and we would also know if we were more careful.

May the Lord grant us revelation; we need discernment; we need intuition. It is the life inside. It is salvation inside, cleansing, filling; it is all inside. Revelation is inside. It is for exhibition outside, but always remember that it is inside. God's Son said as much when He said, "The pure in heart will see God." (See Matthew 5:8.) There is an inward sight of God, and it is the pure in heart who see God.

Lord, keep us pure so that we will never block the way.

LOVE

Love is always in the place of revelation.

Though I speak with the tongues of men and of angels, but have not love, I have become sounding brass or a clanging cymbal. And though I have the gift of prophecy, and understand all mysteries and all knowledge, and though I have all faith, so that I could remove mountains, but have not love, I am nothing.

(1 Corinthians 13:1–2)

Now, it is a remarkable fact that God intends us to be examples of the truth. These are divine truths, and God intends us to be examples of these truths. Beloved, it is lovely to be in the will of God. Now then, how may we be something? By just being nothing, by receiving the Holy Spirit, by being in the place where you can be operated by God and filled with the power to operate.

What it must be to have speaking ability, to have a beautiful language, as so many men have! There are men who are wonderful in language. I used to like to read Talmadge when he was alive; how his messages used to inspire me. But, oh, this divine power! It is wonderful to have the tongue of an angel so that all the people who hear you are moved by your use of language. Yet how I would weep, how my heart would be broken, if I came to speak before you in beautiful language without the power!

If I had an angel's language and the people were all taken with what I said, but Jesus was not glorified at all, it would all be hopeless, barren, and unfruitful. I myself should be nothing. But if I speak and say, "Lord, let them hear Your voice. Lord, let them be compelled to hear Your truth. Lord, anyhow, any way, hide me today," then He becomes glorious, and all the people say, "We have seen Jesus!"

When I was in California, I spent many days with our dear Brother Montgomery when I had a chance. During this time, a man wrote to Brother Montgomery. This man had been saved but had lost his joy; he had lost all he had. He wrote, "I am through with everything. I am not going to touch this thing again; I am through." Brother Montgomery wrote back to him and said, "I will never try to persuade you again if you will hear once. There is a man from England, and if you will only hear him once, I will pay all your expenses." So he came. He listened, and at the end of the time he said to me, "This is the truth I am telling you. I have seen the Lord standing beside you, and I heard His voice. I never even saw you.

"I have a lot of money," he continued, "and I have a valley five hundred miles long. If you speak the word to me, I will go on your word, and I will open that valley for the Lord."

I have preached in several of his places, and God has used him wonderfully to speak throughout that valley. What I would have missed when he came the first day, if I had been trying to say something of my own instead of the Lord being there and speaking His words through me! Never let us do anything to lose this divine love, this close affection in our hearts that says, "Not I, but Christ; not I, but Christ!"

I want to say, "Forget yourself and get lost in Him." Lose all your identity in the Son of God. Let Him become all in all. Seek only the Lord, and let Him be glorified. You will have gifts; you will have grace and wisdom. God is waiting for the person who will lay all on the altar, fifty-two weeks in the year, three hundred and sixty-five days in the year, and then continue perpetually in the Holy Spirit.

I would have liked to have gone on with this topic. I have such joy in this. Beloved, go on for every blessing from the Lord, so that the Lord will be large in you, so that the wood and the hay and the stubble will be burned up (see 1 Corinthians 3:12–13 KJV), and the Lord will bring you to a great harvest time. Now, beloved, shall we not present ourselves to the Lord so that He may put His hand upon us and say, "My child, my child, be obedient to the message; hear what the Spirit says to you so that you may go on and possess the land"? The Lord will give you a great inheritance.

Smith Wigglesworth Only Believe

22

Full of the Holy Spirit

Jesus says, *"Do not be afraid; only believe"* (Mark 5:36). The people in whom God delights are the ones who rest upon His Word without wavering. God has nothing for the man who doubts, for *"let not that man suppose that he will receive anything from the Lord"* (James 1:7). Therefore, I would like us to get this verse deep down into our hearts, until it penetrates every fiber of our being: *"Only believe!"* We know that *"all things are possible"* (Matthew 19:26). *"Only believe."*

God has a plan for this meeting, beyond anything that we have ever known before. He has a plan for every individual life, and if we have any other plan in view, we miss the grandest plan of all! Nothing in the past is equal to the present, and nothing in the present can equal the things of tomorrow, for tomorrow should be so filled with holy expectations that we will be living flames for God. God never intended His people to be ordinary or commonplace.

His intentions were that they should be on fire for Him, conscious of His divine power, realizing the glory of the cross that foreshadows the crown.

THE STORY OF STEPHEN

God has given me a very special Scripture to share:

Now in those days, when the number of the disciples was multiplying, there arose a complaint against the Hebrews by the Hellenists, because their widows were neglected in the daily distribution. Then the twelve summoned the multitude of the disciples and said, "It is not desirable that we should leave the word of God and serve tables. Therefore, brethren, seek out from among you seven men of good reputation, full of the Holy Spirit and wisdom, whom we may appoint over this business." ...And the saying pleased the whole multitude. And they chose Stephen, a man full of faith and the Holy Spirit, and Philip, Prochorus, Nicanor, Timon, Parmenas, and Nicolas, a proselyte from Antioch. (Acts 6:1–3, 5)

During the time of the early church, the disciples were hard-pressed in all areas. The things of the natural life could not be attended to, and many were complaining about the neglect of their widows. The disciples therefore decided on a plan, which was to choose seven men to do the work—men who were "full of the Holy Spirit." What a divine thought! No matter what kind of work was to be done, however menial it may have been, the person chosen had to be filled with the Holy Spirit. The plan of the church was that everything, even the things of the natural life, had to be sanctified unto God, for the church had to be a Holy Spirit church.

Beloved, God has never ordained anything less! There is one thing that I want to stress in these meetings; that is, no matter what else may happen, first and foremost, I want to emphasize these questions: "Have you received the Holy Spirit since you believed?" (See Acts 19:2 KJV.) "Are you filled with divine power?" This is the heritage of the church, to be so clothed with power that God can lay His hand on any member at any time to do His perfect will.

There is no stopping in the Spirit-filled life. We begin at the cross—the place of ignominy, shame, and death—and that very death brings the power of resurrection life. And, being filled with the Holy Spirit, we go on *"from glory to glory"* (2 Corinthians 3:18). Let us not forget that possessing the baptism in the Holy Spirit means that there must be an ever increasing holiness in us.

How the church needs divine anointing—God's presence and power so manifested that the world will know it! People know when the tide is flowing; they also know when it is ebbing.

The necessity that seven men be chosen for the position of serving tables was very evident. The disciples knew that these seven men were men ready for active service, and so they chose them. In Acts 6:5, we read, *"And the saying pleased the whole multitude. And they chose Stephen, a man full of faith and the Holy Spirit, and Philip."* There were five others listed, of course, but Stephen and Philip stand out most prominently in the Scriptures. Philip was a man so filled with the Holy Spirit that a revival always followed wherever he went. Stephen was a man so filled with divine power that, although serving tables might have been all right in the minds of the other disciples, God had a greater vision for him—a baptism of fire, of power and divine anointing, that took him on and on to the climax of his life, until he saw right into the open heavens.

Had we been there with the disciples at that time, I believe we would have heard them saying to each other, "Look here! Neither Stephen nor Philip are doing the work we called them to. If they do not attend to business, we will have to get someone else!" That was the natural way of thinking, but divine order is far above our finite planning. When we please God in our daily activities, we will always find in operation the fact that *"he who is faithful in what is least* [God will make] *faithful also in much"* (Luke 16:10). We have such an example right here—a man chosen to serve tables who had such a revelation of the mind of Christ and of the depth and height of God that there was no pause in his experience, but a going forward with leaps and bounds. Beloved, there is a race to be run; there is a crown to be won; we cannot stand still! I say unto you, *"Be vigilant"* (1 Peter 5:8). Be vigilant! Let no one take your crown! (See Revelation 3:11.)

God has privileged us in Christ Jesus to live above the ordinary human plane of life. Those who want to be ordinary and live on a lower plane can do so, but as for me, I will not! For the same anointing, the same zeal, the same Holy Spirit power that was at the command of Stephen and the apostles is at our command. We have the same God that Abraham had, that Elijah had, and we do not need to come short in any gift or grace. (See 1 Corinthians 1:7.) We may not possess the gifts as abiding gifts, but as we are full of the Holy Spirit and divine anointing, it is possible, when there is need, for God to manifest every gift of the Spirit through us. As I have already said, I do not mean by this that we should necessarily possess the gifts permanently, but there should be a manifestation of the gifts as God may choose to use us.

This ordinary man Stephen became mighty under the Holy Spirit's anointing, and now he stands supreme, in many ways, among the apostles. *"And Stephen, full of faith and power, did great wonders and signs among the people"* (Acts 6:8). As we go deeper in God, He enlarges our understanding and places before us a wide-open door, and I am not surprised that this man chosen to serve tables was afterward called to a higher plane. "What do you mean?" you may ask. "Did he quit this service?" No! But he was lost in the power of God. He lost sight of everything in the natural and steadfastly fixed his gaze upon Jesus, *"the author and finisher of our faith"* (Hebrews 12:2), until he was transformed into a shining light in the kingdom of God.

Oh, that we might be awakened to believe His Word, to understand the mind of the Spirit, for there is an inner place of whiteness and purity where we can see God. Stephen was just as ordinary a person as you and I, but he was in the place where God could so move upon him that he, in turn, could move everything before him. He began in a most humble place and ended in a blaze of glory. Beloved, dare to believe Christ!

RESISTANCE TO THE HOLY SPIRIT

As you go on in this life of the Spirit, you will find that the devil will begin to get restless and there will be a "stir in the synagogue," so to speak. It was so with Stephen. Any number of people may be found in the church who are very proper in a worldly sense—always properly dressed, the elite of the land, welcoming into the church everything but the power of God. Let us read what God says about them:

Then there arose some from what is called the Synagogue of the Freedmen (Cyrenians, Alexandrians, and those from Cilicia and Asia), disputing with Stephen. And they were not able to resist the wisdom and the Spirit by which he spoke.

(Acts 6:9–10)

The Freedmen could not stand the truth of God. With these opponents, Stephen found himself in the same predicament as the blind man whom Jesus had healed. (See John 9:1–34.) As soon as the blind man's eyes were opened, the religious leaders shut him out of the synagogue. They would not have anybody in the synagogue with his eyes open. It is the same today; as soon as you receive spiritual eyesight, out you go!

These Freedmen, Cyrenians, and Alexandrians rose up full of wrath in the very place where they should have been full of the power of God, full of divine love, and full of reverence for the Holy Spirit. They rose up against Stephen, this man who was *"full of the Holy Spirit"* (Acts 6:3).

Beloved, if there is anything in your life that in any way resists the power of the Holy Spirit and the entrance of His Word into your heart and life, drop on your knees and cry out loud for mercy! When the Spirit of God is brooding over your heart's door, do not resist Him. Open your heart to the touch of God. There is a resisting of and a *"striving against sin"* that leads even *"to bloodshed"* (Hebrews 12:4), and there is also a resisting of the Holy Spirit that will drive you into sin.

Stephen spoke with remarkable wisdom. Where he was, things began to move. You will find that there is always a moving when the Holy Spirit has control. These people were brought under conviction by the message of Stephen, but they resisted; they did anything and everything to stifle that conviction. Not only did they lie, but they got others to lie against this man, who would have laid down his life for any one of them. Stephen had been used by God to heal the sick and to perform miracles, yet they brought false accusations against him. What effect did their accusations have on Stephen? *"And all who sat in the council, looking steadfastly at him, saw his face as the face of an angel"* (Acts 6:15).

Something had happened in the life of this man chosen for menial service, and he had become mighty for God. How was it accomplished in him? It was because his aim was high. Faithful in little, Stephen was brought by God to full fruition. Under the inspiration of divine power, by which he spoke, his opponents could not help but listen. Even the angels listened, for he spoke with holy, prophetic utterance before that council. Beginning with Abraham and Moses, he continued unfolding the truth. What a marvelous exhortation! Take your Bibles and read the seventh chapter of Acts; "listen in" as the angels listened in. As light upon light, truth upon truth, revelation upon revelation found its way into his opponents' calloused hearts; they gazed at Stephen in astonishment. Perhaps their hearts became warm at times, and they may have said, "Truly, this man is sent by God." But then he hurled at them the truth:

> You stiffnecked and uncircumcised in heart and ears! You always resist the Holy Spirit; as your fathers did, so do you. Which of the prophets did your fathers not persecute? And they killed those who foretold the coming of the Just One, of whom you now have become the betrayers and murderers, who have received the law by the direction of angels and have not kept it.
>
> (Acts 7:51–53)

Then what happened? These men were moved; they were *"cut to the heart, and they gnashed at him with their teeth"* (verse 54).

There are two marvelous occasions in the Scriptures where the people were "cut to the heart." In the second chapter of the Acts of the Apostles, in the thirty-seventh verse, after Peter had delivered that inspired sermon on the Day of Pentecost, the people were *"cut to the heart"* with conviction, and three thousand souls were added to the church.

Then, here is Stephen, speaking under the inspiration of the Holy Spirit, and the men of this council, being "cut to the heart," rose up as one man to slay him. As you go down through this seventh chapter of Acts, starting with the fifty-fifth verse, what a picture you have before you! As I close my eyes, I can get a vision of this scene in every detail—the howling mob with their revengeful, murderous spirit, ready to devour this holy man, and he, *"being full of the Holy Spirit"* (verse 55), gazing steadfastly into heaven. What did he see there? From his place of helplessness, he looked up and said, *"Look! I see the heavens opened and the Son of Man standing at the right hand of God!"* (verse 56).

Is that the position that Jesus went to heaven to take? No! He went to sit at the right hand of the Father. But on behalf of the first martyr, on behalf of the man with that burning flame of Holy Spirit power, God's Son stood up in honorary testimony of him who was first called to serve tables and was faithful unto death.

But is that all? No! I am so glad that that is not all. As the stones came flying at Stephen, pounding his body, crashing into his bones, striking his head, mangling his beautiful face, what happened? How did this scene end? With a sublime, upward look, this man, chosen for an ordinary task but filled with the Holy Spirit, was so moved upon by God that he finished his earthly work in a blaze of glory, magnifying God with his last breath. Looking up into the face of the Master, he said, *"'Lord, do not charge them with this sin.' And when he had said this, he fell asleep"* (Acts 7:60).

Friends, it is worth dying a thousand deaths to gain that spirit. What a divine ending to the life and testimony of a man who had been chosen to serve tables.

23

Called to Serve

W e are a very wealthy and privileged people to be able to gather together to worship the Lord. I count it a very holy thing to gather together to think of Him, because it is impossible to think of Him and be in any way unholy. The very thought of Jesus will confirm truth and righteousness and power in your mortal body. There is something very remarkable about Him. When John saw Him, the impression that he had was that He was the *"lamb without blemish and without spot"* (1 Peter 1:19). When God speaks about Jesus, He says, *"He came forth in the brightness of the expression of the countenance of God."* When revelation comes, it says, *"In Him dwells all the fullness"* (Colossians 2:9). His character is beautiful. His display of meekness is lovely. His compassion is greater than that of anyone in all of humanity. He felt infirmities. He helps those who pass through trials. And it is to be said about Him what is not said about anyone else: "[He] *was in all points tempted as we are, yet without sin*" (Hebrews 4:15).

I want you, as the author of Hebrews wonderfully said, to "*consider Him who endured such hostility from sinners against Himself, lest you become weary and discouraged in your souls*" (Hebrews 12:3). When you are weary and tempted and tried and all men are against you, consider Him who has passed through it all, so that He might be able to help you in the trial as you are passing through it. He will sustain you in the strife. When all things seem to indicate that you have failed, the Lord of Hosts, the God of Jacob, the salvation of our Christ will so reinforce you that you will be stronger than any concrete building that was ever made.

AN INTERPRETATION OF TONGUES:

Your God, your Lord, in whom you trust, will make you so strong in the Lord and in the power of His might that no evil thing will befall you. As He was with Moses, He will be with you. As He stood by Daniel, He will cause the lions' mouths to close. He will shut up all that is against you; and the favor of heaven, the smile of the Most High, the kiss of His love, will make you know you are covered with the Dove.

OUR CALLING

The following Scripture is so beautiful: "*I, therefore, the prisoner of the Lord, beseech you to walk worthy of the calling with which you were called*" (Ephesians 4:1). Paul, who spoke to us in this verse, was an example for the church. He was filled with the loveliness of the character of the Master through the Spirit's power. He was zealous that we may walk worthy. This is the day of calling that he spoke about; this is the opportunity of our lifetime. This is the place where God increases strength or opens the door of a new way of ministry so that we will come into like-mindedness with this holy apostle who was a prisoner.

LOWLINESS AND MEEKNESS

The passage goes on to say, *"With all lowliness and gentleness, with longsuffering, bearing with one another in love"* (Ephesians 4:2).

Jesus emphasized the new commandment when He left us: *"A new commandment I give to you, that you love one another; as I have loved you, that you also love one another"* (John 13:34). To the extent that we miss this instruction, we miss all the Master's instruction. If we miss that commandment, we miss everything. All the future summits of glory are yours in the very fact that you have been recreated in a deeper order by that commandment He gave us.

When we reach this attitude of love, then we make no mistake about lowliness. We will submit ourselves in the future in order that we may be useful to one another. The greatest plan that Jesus ever presented in His ministry was the ministry of service. He said, *"I am among you as the One who serves"* (Luke 22:27). And when we come to a place where we serve for pure love's sake, because it is the divine hand of the Master upon us, we will find out that we will never fail. Love never fails when it is divinely appointed in us. However, the so-called love in our human nature does fail and has failed from the beginning.

Suppose a man corresponds with me, seeking to learn more about me and to establish a relationship. The only thing I would have to say in answering his letters is, "Brother, all that I know about

Wigglesworth is bad." There is no good thing in human nature. However, all that I know about the new creation in Wigglesworth is good. The important thing is whether we are living in the old creation or the new creation. So I implore you to see that there is a lowliness, a humbleness, that leads you to meekness, that leads you to separate yourself from the world, that puts you so in touch with the Master that you know you are touching God. The blood of Jesus cleanses you from sin and all pollution. (See 1 John 1:7.) There is something in this holy position that makes you know you are free from the power of the Enemy.

We have yet to see the forcefulness of the Word of God. I refer to it in passing, as described in Hebrews:

> *For the word of God is living and powerful, and sharper than any two-edged sword, piercing even to the division of soul and spirit, and of joints and marrow, and is a discerner of the thoughts and intents of the heart.* (Hebrews 4:12)

The Word, the life, the presence, the power, is in your body, in the very marrow of your bones, and absolutely everything else must be discharged. Sometimes we do not fully reflect on this wonderful truth: the Word, the life, the Christ who is the Word, separates your soul from your spirit. What a wonderful work! The Spirit divides you from soul affection, from human weakness, from all depravity. The blood of Jesus can cleanse your blood until your very soul is purified and your very nature is destroyed by the nature of the living Christ.

I am speaking to you about resurrection touches. In Christ, we have encountered divine resurrection touches. In the greatest work God ever did on the face of the earth, He had to use His operation power: Christ was raised from the dead by the operation of the power of God. As the resurrection of Christ operates in our hearts, it will dethrone the wrong things. And at the same time that it dethrones, it will build the right things. Callousness will have to change; hardness will have to disappear; all evil thoughts will have to go. And in the place of these will be lowliness of mind.

What beautiful cooperation with God in thought and power and holiness! The Master *"made Himself of no reputation"* (Philippians 2:7). He absolutely left the glory of heaven, with all its wonder. He left it and submitted Himself to humiliation. He went down, down, down into death for one purpose only: that He might destroy the power of death, even the devil, and deliver those people who all their lifetime have been subject to fear—deliver them from the fear of death and the devil. (See Hebrews 2:14–15.)

This is a wonderful plan for us. But how will it come to pass? By transformation, resurrection, thoughts of holiness, intense zeal, desire for all of God, until we live and move in the atmosphere of holiness.

If I say "holiness" or "baptism" or "resurrection" or "rapture," remember that all these words are tremendous. And there is another phrase I would like to emphasize: *"After you were illuminated"* (Hebrews 10:32). Have you been to the place of illumination? What does the word mean? Illumination means this: that your very mind, which was depraved, is now the mind of Christ; the very nature that was bound now has a resurrection touch; your very body has come in contact with the life of God until you who were lost are found, and you who were dead are alive again by the resurrection power of the Word of the life of Christ. What a glorious inheritance in the Spirit!

Have you come to this place? Don't forget the ladder that Jacob saw. (See Genesis 28:10–22.) As I was nearing Jerusalem and saw the city for the first time, someone said to me, "See that place there? That is where Jacob saw the ladder that reached from earth to heaven."

Believer, if you have not reached all this, the ladder extends from heaven to earth to take you from earth to heaven. Do not be afraid of taking the steps. You will not slip back. Have faith in God. Experience divine resurrection life—more divine in thought, more wonderful in revelation. Resurrection life means living in the Spirit, wakened into all likeness, made alive by the same Spirit!

AN INTERPRETATION OF TONGUES:

He rose, and in His rising, He lifted us and He placed us in the place of seating, and then gave us a holy language, and then began to entertain us and show in us that now the body is His and that we become members in particular of the body. Sometimes He chastens us so that all the dross might go and all the wood and the stubble might be burned in the testing, so that He might get purer gold, purer life, purer soul, so that there should be nothing in the body that should be defiling, but He should take us out of the world and make us like a ripe shock of corn, ready for the dawning of the morning.

Are you lowly and meek in your mind? It is the divine plan of the Savior. You must be like Him. Do you desire to be like Him? There is nothing but yourself that can hinder you in this. You are the one who stops the current. You are the one who stops the life. The river and the current are coming just now; I feel them all over me.

While ministering in one place, we had a banquet for people who were distressed—people who were lame and weary, blind and diseased in every way. We had a big crowd of people, and we fed them all.

After we got them well filled with all the good things that were provided, we said, "Now we are going to give you some entertainment."

A man who had spent many years in a wheelchair but had been healed came onto the platform and told how he had been set free. A person who had suffered from a hemorrhage for many years came and testified. A blind man came and told how his eyes had been opened. For one hour, the people were entertained.

Then I said to the people, "Are you ready?"

Oh, they were all so ready! A dear man got hold of a boy who was encased in iron from top to bottom, lifted him up, and placed him onto the platform. Hands were laid upon him in the name of Jesus.

"Papa! Papa! Papa!" the boy said. "It's going all over me! Oh, Papa, come and take these irons off!" I do like to hear children speak; they say such wonderful things. The father took the irons off, and the life of God had gone all over the boy!

This is what I feel: the life of God going all over me, the power of God all over me. Don't you know this is the resurrection touch? This is the divine life; this is what God has brought us into. Let it go over us, Lord—the power of the Holy Spirit, the resurrection of heaven, the sweetness of Your blessing, the joy of the Lord!

If our fellowship below with Jesus be so sweet,

What heights of rapture shall we know

When round His throne we meet!

AN INTERPRETATION OF TONGUES:

The Spirit sweetly falls like the dew, just as still on the grass, and as it comes, it is for a purpose—God's purpose. It may be withered grass, but God calls it to come forth again. And the Spirit of the Lord is right in the midst of you this morning. Though you might have been withered, dried, and barren for a long time, the dew is falling. God is in the midst of us with His spirit of revival, and He is saying to you, "All things are possible; only believe," and He will change you.

THE UNITY OF THE SPIRIT

"Endeavoring to keep the unity of the Spirit in the bond of peace" (Ephesians 4:3).

You are bound forever out of loyalty to God to see that no division comes into the church body, to see that nothing comes into the assembly, as it came into David's flock, to tear and rend the body. You have to be careful. If a person comes along with a prophecy and you find that it is tearing down and bringing trouble, denounce it accordingly; judge it by the Word. You will find that all true prophecy will be perfectly full of hopefulness. It will have compassion; it will have comfort; it will have edification. So if anything comes into the church that you know is hurting the flock and disturbing the assembly, you must see to it that you begin to pray so that this thing is put to death. Bring unity in the bonds of perfection so that the church of God will receive edification. Then the church will begin to be built up in the faith and the establishing of truth, and believers will be one.

Do not forget that God means for us to be very faithful to the church so that we do not allow anything to come into the church to break up the body. You cannot find anything in the body in its relation to Christ that has schism in it. Christ's life in the body— there is no schism in that. When Christ's life comes into the church, there will be no discord; there will be a perfect blending of heart and hand, and it will be lovely. Endeavor *"to keep the unity of the Spirit in the bond of peace"* (Ephesians 4:3).

ONE BODY

Now I come to a very important point: *"There is one body"* (verse 4).

There is one body. Recognize that fact. When schism comes into the body, believers always act as though there were more than one. For instance, there is the Wesleyan Church, there is the Baptist Church, and there are many other churches. What do I need to notice about them? I have to see that right in that body, right in that church, God has a remnant belonging to His body. All the members of that church may not be of the body, but God has a remnant in that church. I should not go out and denounce the Baptists, the Wesleyans, or any other church. What I need to do, what I must do, is to so live in the Spirit of Christ that they will see that I am one with them. It is the Holy Spirit in the new church, in the body, the spiritual body, who is uniting, binding, and mightily moving. In every church, whether that church baptizes or not, there is a place where the Spirit is.

Now, beloved, the baptism of the Spirit is to be planted deeper and deeper in us until there is not a part that is left, and the manifestation of the power of the new creation by the Holy Spirit is right in our mortal bodies. Where we once were, He now reigns supreme, manifesting the very Christ inside of us, the Holy Spirit fulfilling all things right there.

Jesus has been wonderfully ordained; He has been incarnated by God, and God has given Him preeminence. He has to be preeminent in us. And someday we will see the preeminence of this wonderful Savior, and we will take our crowns and place them at His feet. Then He will put the Father in all preeminence and will take all our crowns and us also and present us to the Father, with Himself, so that the Father will be all in all, forever and ever.

That will take ten million years. In thinking about it, my calculation is that the Marriage and the Supper of the Lamb will take fifty million years. "What do you mean?" you ask. *"With the Lord one day is as a thousand years"* (2 Peter 3:8). Our supernatural bodies, in the glory of their infinite relationship, will so live in the bliss of heaven that time will fly. The Supper and the Marriage will be supremely delightful and full and refreshing, pure and glorious and light. Oh, hallelujah! It is coming! It is not past; it is on the way. It is a glory we have yet to enter into.

ONE LORD AND ONE FAITH

There is one body and one Spirit, just as you were called in one hope of your calling; one Lord, one faith, one baptism.
(Ephesians 4:4–5)

"One Lord." Oh, it is lovely! One Lord, one heart, one love, one association. *"One Lord, one faith, one baptism."* It is the baptism of the Spirit, the baptism of the new creation order, the baptism into

divine life, the baptism with fire, the baptism with zeal, the baptism with passion, the baptism with inward travail. Oh, it is a baptism indeed! Jesus had it. He travailed; He acted with compassion.

"One Lord." We are all one, all in Christ Jesus, all one in Christ. We have *"one faith,"* which lays hold of the immensities, which dares to believe, which holds fast to what we have, so that no one may take our crowns. (See Revelation 3:11.) For we are being quickened by this resurrection, and now faith lays hold.

Contend for eternal life. Lay hold of it—eternal life! It is something we cannot handle, something we cannot see, yet it is more real than we are. Lay hold of it. Let no man rob you of it. It is a crown; it is a position in the Holy One. It is a place of identification. It is a place of Him bringing you into order. Only He can do it—and He does it.

THE GOD WHO IS OVER ALL

Let us look at the next verse, which is very beautiful, for here is our position in this world: *"One God and Father of all, who is above all, and through all, and in you all"* (Ephesians 4:6).

"Who is above all." Think of that! It does not matter what the Enemy may bring to you, or try to bring; remember, the Father, who is above all, is over you. Is there anything else? Yes, the next thought is larger still: *"Through all."* And the next: *"In you all."* The God of power, majesty, and glory can bring you to a place of dethroning everything else! The Father of all is *"above all, and through all, and in you all."*

Do you dare to believe it? You should go away with such inspiration in the area of faith that you will never have a doubt again, and I want above all things to take you to that place.

Remember, God our Father is so intensely desirous to have all the fullness of the manifestation of His power, that we do not have to have one thing that His Son did not come to bring. We have to have perfect redemption; we have to know all the powers of righteousness; we have to understand perfectly that we are brought to the place where He is with us in all power, dethroning the power of the Enemy.

God over you—that is real. The God who is over you is more than a million times greater than the devil, than the powers of evil, than the powers of darkness. How do I know? Hear what the devil said to God about Job: *"Have You not made a hedge around him?"* (Job 1:10). This verse means that the devil was unable to get near Job because there was a hedge. What was the hedge? It was the almighty power of God. It was not a thorny hedge; it was not a hedge of thistles. It was the presence of the Lord all around Job. And the presence of the Lord Almighty is so around us that the devil cannot break through that wonderful covering.

The devil is against the living Christ and wants to destroy Him, and if you are filled with the living Christ, the devil is eager to get you out of the way in order to destroy Christ's power. Say this to the Lord: "Now, Lord, look after this property of yours." Then the devil cannot get near you. When does he get near? When you dethrone Christ, ignoring His rightful position over you, in you, and through you.

You will be strong if you believe this truth. I preach faith, and I know it will carry you through if you dare to believe. Faith is the victory—always. Glory to Jesus!

THE GIFTS OF CHRIST

Notice next that the apostle Paul received revelation about Jesus. He spoke about the grace and the gifts of Christ—not the gifts of the Holy Spirit, but the gifts of Christ: *"But to each one of us grace was given according to the measure of Christ's gift"* (Ephesians 4:7).

The gifts of Christ are so different from the gifts of the Holy Spirit that I want to explain this for a moment:

> *Therefore He says, "When He ascended on high, He led captivity captive, and gave gifts to men."...And He Himself gave some to be apostles, some prophets, some evangelists, and some pastors and teachers, for the equipping of the saints for the work of ministry, for the edifying of the body of Christ.*
>
> (Ephesians 4:8, 11–12)

These verses are in the Epistles. The Gospels are the gospel of the kingdom. In the Acts of the Apostles, those who believed repented, were saved, were baptized, and became eligible to come into the Epistles, so that they might be in the body as is described in the Epistles. The body is not made up after you get into the Epistles; you are joined to the body the moment you believe.

For instance, some of you may have children, and they have different names, but the moment they appeared in the world, they were in your family. The moment they were born, they became a part of your family.

The moment you are born of God, you are in the family, and you are in the body, as He is in the body, and you are in the body collectively and particularly. After you come into the body, then the body has to receive the sealing of the promise, or the fulfillment of promise, that is, that Christ will be in you, reigning in you mightily. The Holy Spirit will come to unveil the King in all His glory so that He might reign as King there, the Holy Spirit serving in every way to make Him King.

You are in the body. The Holy Spirit gives gifts in the body. Living in this holy order, you may find that revelation comes to you and makes you a prophet. Some of you may have a clear understanding that you have been called into apostleship. Some of you may have perfect knowledge that you are to be pastors. When you come to be sealed with the Spirit of promise, then you find out that Jesus is pleased and gives gifts, in order that the church might come into a perfect position of being so blended together that there could be no division. Jesus wants His church to be a perfect body—perfect in stature, perfect in oneness in Him.

I have been speaking to this end: that you may see the calling that Paul was speaking about—humility of mind, meekness of spirit, knowing that God is in you and through you, knowing that the power of the Spirit is mightily bringing you to the place where not only the gifts of the Spirit but also the gifts of Christ have been given to you, making you eligible for the great work you have to do.

My purpose in this teaching was not to tell what God has for you in the future. Press in now, and claim your rights. Let the Lord Jesus be so glorified that He will make you fruit-bearers— strong in power, giving glory to God, having *"no confidence in the flesh"* (Philippians 3:3) but being separated from natural things, now in the Spirit, living fully in the will of God.

24

The Flood Tide

The increase of God. (Colossians 2:19 KJV)

Wherever Jesus went, the multitudes followed Him, because He
lived, moved, breathed, was swallowed up, clothed, and filled
by God. He was God; and as the Son of Man, the Spirit of God—
the Spirit of creative holiness—rested upon Him. It is lovely to be
holy. Jesus came to impart to us the Spirit of holiness.

We are only at the edge of things; the almighty plan for the
future is marvelous. God must do something to increase. We need
a revival to revive all we touch within us and outside of us. We need
a flood tide with a deluge behind it. Jesus left one hundred twenty
men to turn the world upside down. The Spirit is upon us to change
our situation. We must move on; we must let God increase in us for
the deliverance of multitudes; and we must travail until souls are
born and quickened into a new relationship with heaven. Jesus had

divine authority with power, and He left it for us. We must preach truth, holiness, and purity *"in the inward parts"* (Psalm 51:6).

> *You have loved righteousness and hated lawlessness; therefore God, Your God, has anointed You with the oil of gladness more than Your companions.* (Hebrews 1:9)

I am thirsty for more of God. He was not only holy, but He loved holiness.

AN INTERPRETATION OF TONGUES:

It is the depths that God gets into that we may reflect Him and manifest a life having Christ enthroned in the heart, drinking into a new fullness, new intuition, for as He is, so are we in this world.

Jesus trod the winepress alone (see Isaiah 63:3), despising the cross and the shame. He bore it all alone so that we might be *"partakers of the divine nature"* (2 Peter 1:4), sharers in the divine plan of holiness. That's revival—Jesus manifesting divine authority. He was without sin. People saw the Lamb of God in a new way. Hallelujah! Let us live in holiness, and revival will come down, and God will enable us to do the work to which we are appointed. All Jesus said came to pass: signs, wonders, mighty deeds. Only believe, and yield and yield, until all the vision is fulfilled.

A MIGHTY FAITH

God has a design, a purpose, a rest of faith. We are saved by faith and kept by faith. Faith is substance; it is also evidence. (See Hebrews 11:1.) God is! He is! And *"He is a rewarder of those who diligently seek Him"* (verse 6). We are to testify, to bear witness to what we know. To know that we know is a wonderful position to be in.

AN INTERPRETATION OF TONGUES:

The Lord is the great promoter of divine possibility, pressing you into the attitude of daring to believe all that the Word says. We are to be living words, epistles of Christ, known and read of all men. The revelation of Christ, past and future; in Him all things consist. He is in us.

We are living in the inheritance of faith because of the grace of God. We are saved for eternity by the operation of the Spirit, who brings forth unto God. Heaven is brought to earth until God quickens all things into beauty, manifesting His power in living witnesses. God is in us for the world, so that the world may be blessed. We need power to lay hold of Omnipotence and to impart to others the Word of Life. This is a new epoch with new vision and new power. Christ in us is greater than we know. All things are possible if you dare to believe. The treasure is in earthen vessels so that Jesus may be glorified. (See 2 Corinthians 4:7.)

Let us go forth bringing glory to God. Faith is substance, a mightiness of reality, a deposit of divine nature, the creative God within. The moment you believe, you are clothed with a new power to lay hold of possibility and make it reality. The people said to Jesus, *"Lord, give us this bread always"* (John 6:34). Jesus said, *"He who feeds on Me will live because of Me"* (verse 57).

Have the faith of God. The man who comes into great association with God needs a heavenly measure. Faith is the greatest of all. We are saved by a new life, the Word of God, an association with the living Christ. A new creation continually takes us into new revelation.

THE LIFE OF GOD WITHIN US

In the beginning was the Word, and the Word was with God, and the Word was God. …All things were made through Him, and without Him nothing was made that was made.

(John 1:1, 3)

All was made by the Word. I am begotten by His Word. There is a substance within me that has almighty power in it if I dare to believe. Faith goes on to be an act, a reality, a deposit of God, an almighty flame moving me to act, so that signs and wonders are manifested. I have a living faith within my earthen body.

Are you begotten? Is faith an act within you? Some need a touch; some are captives and need liberty. As many as Jesus touched were made perfectly whole. Faith takes you to the place where God reigns and you drink from His bountiful store. Unbelief is sin, for Jesus went to death to bring us the light of life.

Jesus asked, *"Are you able to drink the cup that I am about to drink, and be baptized with the baptism that I am baptized with?"* (Matthew 20:22). The cup and the baptism are a joined position. You cannot live if you want to bring everything into life. His life is manifested power overflowing. We must decrease if the life of God is to be manifested. (See John 3:30.) There is not room for two kinds of life in one body. Death for life—that is the price to pay for the manifested power of God through you. As you die to human desire, there comes a fellowship within, perfected cooperation, you ceasing, God increasing. God in you is a living substance, a spiritual nature. You live by another life, the faith of the Son of God.

AN INTERPRETATION OF TONGUES:

The Spirit, He breathed through and quickens until the body is a temple exhibiting Jesus—His life, His freshness, a new life divine. Paul said, "Christ lives in me, and the life I live in the flesh I live by faith."

As the Holy Spirit reveals Jesus, He is real—the living Word, effective, acting, speaking, thinking, praying, and singing. Oh, it is a wonderful life, this substance of the Word of God, which includes possibility and opportunity. *"Greater is he that is in you"* (1 John 4:4 kjv). Paul said, *"When I am weak, then I am strong"* (2 Corinthians 12:10).

Jesus walked in supremacy; He lived in the kingdom. And God will take us through because of Calvary. He has given us power over all the power of the enemy. (See Luke 10:19.) He won it for us at Calvary. All must be subject to His power. What should we do to work the works? *"This is the work of God, that you believe"* (John 6:29). Whatsoever He says will come to pass. That is God's Word.

A frail, weak man with sunken cheeks said to me, "Can you help me?" Beloved, there is not one who cannot be helped. God has opened the doors for us to let Him manifest signs and wonders. The authority is inside, not outside.

Could I help him? He had been fed liquid food through a tube for three months. I said, "Go home and eat a good supper." He did, and woke up to find the tube hole closed up. God knew he did not need two holes to eat by.

We must remain in a strong, resolute resting on the authority of God's Word. We must have one great desire and purpose: to do what He says. We must live in this holy Word, rejoicing in the manifestation of the life of God on behalf of the sick and perishing multitudes. Amen.

Ever Increasing Faith

25

The Power of the Name

Now as the lame man who was healed held on to Peter and John, all the people ran together to them in the porch which is called Solomon's, greatly amazed. So when Peter saw it, he responded to the people: "Men of Israel, why do you marvel at this? Or why look so intently at us, as though by our own power or godliness we had made this man walk? The God of Abraham, Isaac, and Jacob, the God of our fathers, glorified His Servant Jesus, whom you delivered up and denied in the presence of Pilate, when he was determined to let Him go. But you denied the Holy One and the Just, and asked for a murderer to be granted to you, and killed the Prince of life, whom God raised from the dead, of which we are witnesses. And His name, through faith in His name, has made this man strong, whom you see and know. Yes, the faith which comes through Him has given him this perfect soundness in the presence of you all."

(Acts 3:11–16)

All things are possible through the name of Jesus. (See Matthew 19:26.) *"God also has highly exalted Him and given Him the name which is above every name, that at the name of Jesus every knee should bow"* (Philippians 2:9–10). There is power to overcome everything in the world through the name of Jesus. I am looking forward to a wonderful union through the name of Jesus. *"There is no other name under heaven given among men by which we must be saved"* (Acts 4:12).

SPEAKING THE NAME OF JESUS

I want to instill in you a sense of the power, the virtue, and the glory of that name. Six people went into the house of a sick man to pray for him. He was a leader in the Episcopal Church, and he lay in his bed utterly helpless, without even strength to help himself. He had read a little tract about healing and had heard about people praying for the sick. So he sent for these friends, who, he thought, could pray *"the prayer of faith"* (James 5:15). He was anointed according to James 5:14, but because he had no immediate manifestation of healing, he wept bitterly. The six people walked out of the room, somewhat crestfallen to see the man lying there in an unchanged condition.

When they were outside, one of the six said, "There is one thing we could have done. I wish you would all go back with me and try it." They all went back and got together in a group. This brother said, "Let us whisper the name of Jesus." At first, when they whispered this worthy name, nothing seemed to happen. But as they continued to whisper "Jesus! Jesus! Jesus!" the power began to fall. When they saw that God was beginning to work, their faith and joy increased, and they whispered the name louder and louder. As they did so, the man rose from his bed and dressed himself. The secret was just this: those six people had gotten their eyes off the sick man and were taken up with the Lord Jesus Himself. Their faith grasped the power in His name. Oh, if people would only appreciate the power in this name, there is no telling what would happen.

I know that through His name and through the power of His name we have access to God. The very face of Jesus fills the whole place with glory. All over the world there are people magnifying that name, and oh, what a joy it is for me to utter it.

RAISING LAZARUS

One day I went up into the mountains to pray. I had a wonderful day. I was on one of the high mountains of Wales. I had heard of one man going up onto this mountain to pray and the Spirit of the Lord meeting him so wonderfully that his face shone like that of an angel when he returned. Everyone in the village was talking about it. As I went up onto this mountain and spent the day in the presence of the Lord, His wonderful power seemed to envelop and saturate and fill me.

Two years before this time, there had come to our house two lads from Wales. They were just ordinary lads, but they became very zealous for God. They came to our mission and saw some of the works of God. They said to me, "We would not be surprised if the Lord brings you down to Wales to raise our Lazarus." They explained that the leader of their church was a man who had spent his days working in a tin mine and his nights preaching, and the result was that he had collapsed and contracted tuberculosis. For four years he had been a helpless invalid, having to be fed with a spoon.

When I was up on that mountaintop, I was reminded of the Transfiguration (see Matthew 17:1–8), and I felt that the Lord's only purpose in taking us into the glory is to prepare us for greater usefulness in the valley.

INTERPRETATION OF TONGUES

The living God has chosen us for His divine inheritance, and He it is who is preparing us for our ministry, that it may be of God and not of man.

As I was on the mountaintop that day, the Lord said to me, "I want you to go and raise Lazarus."

I told the brother who had accompanied me about this, and when we got down to the valley, I wrote a postcard. It read, "When I was up on the mountain praying today, God told me that I was to go and raise Lazarus." I addressed the postcard to the man whose name had been given to me by the two lads.

When we arrived at the place, we went to the man to whom I had addressed the postcard. He looked at me and asked, "Did you send this?"

"Yes," I replied.

He said, "Do you think we believe in this? Here, take it." And he threw it at me.

The man called a servant and said, "Take this man and show him Lazarus." Then he said to me, "The moment you see him, you will be ready to go home. Nothing will keep you here." And everything he said was true from the natural standpoint. The man was helpless. He was nothing but a mass of bones with skin stretched over them. There was no life to be seen. Everything in him spoke of decay.

I said to him, "Will you shout? You remember that at Jericho the people shouted while the walls were still up. God has a similar victory for you if you will only believe." But I could not get him to believe. There was not an atom of faith there. He had made up his mind not to have anything.

It is a blessed thing to learn that God's Word can never fail. Never listen to human plans. God can work mightily when you persist in believing Him in spite of discouragement from the human standpoint. When I got back to the man to whom I had sent the postcard, he asked, "Are you ready to go now?"

I am not moved by what I see. I am moved only by what I believe. I know this: no man looks at the circumstances if he believes. No man relies on his feelings if he believes. The man who believes God has his request. Every man who comes into the Pentecostal condition can laugh at all things and believe God.

There is something in the Pentecostal work that is different from anything else in the world. Somehow, in Pentecost you know that God is a reality. Wherever the Holy Spirit has the right-of-way, the gifts of the Spirit will be in manifestation. Where these gifts are never in manifestation, I question whether He is present. Pentecostal people are spoiled for anything other than Pentecostal meetings. We want none of the entertainments that other churches are offering. When God comes in, He entertains us Himself. We are entertained by the King of Kings and Lord of Lords! Oh, it is wonderful.

There were difficult conditions in that Welsh village, and it seemed impossible to get the people to believe. "Ready to go home?" I was asked. But a man and a woman there asked us to come and stay with them.

I said to the people, "I want to know how many of you people can pray." No one wanted to pray. I asked if I could get seven people to pray with me for the poor man's deliverance. I said to the two people we were to stay with, "I will count on you two, and there is my friend and myself. We need three others." I told the people I trusted that some of them would awaken to their privilege and come in the morning and join us in prayer for the raising of Lazarus. It will never do to give way to human opinions. If God says a thing, you are to believe it.

I told the people that I would not eat anything that night. When I got to bed, it seemed as if the devil tried to place on me everything that he had placed on that poor man on the sickbed. When I awoke in the middle of the night, I had a cough and all the weakness of a man with tuberculosis. I rolled out of bed onto the floor and cried out to God to deliver me from the power of the devil. I shouted loud enough to wake everybody in the house, but nobody was disturbed. God gave the victory, and I got back into bed again as free as I had ever been in my life. At five o'clock the Lord awakened me and said to me, "Don't break bread until you break it around My table." At six o'clock He gave me these words: *And I will raise him up* (John 6:40).

I elbowed the fellow who was sleeping in the same room. He said, "Ugh!" I elbowed him again and said, "Do you hear? The Lord says He will raise him up."

At eight o'clock they said to me, "Have a little refreshment." But I have found prayer and fasting the greatest joy, and you will always find it so when you are led by God.

When we went to the house where Lazarus lived, there were eight of us altogether. No one can prove to me that God does not always answer prayer. He always does more than that. He always gives *"exceedingly abundantly above all that we ask or think"* (Ephesians 3:20).

I will never forget how the power of God fell on us as we went into that sick man's room. Oh, it was lovely! As we made a circle around the bed, I got one brother to hold the sick man's hand on one side, and I held the other, and we each held the hand of the person next to us. I said, "We are not going to pray; we are just going to use the name of Jesus."

We all knelt down and whispered that one word, "Jesus! Jesus! Jesus!" The power of God fell, and then it lifted. Five times the power of God fell, and then it remained. But the man in the bed was unmoved.

Two years previously, someone had come along and had tried to raise him up, and the devil had used his lack of success as a means of discouraging Lazarus. I said, "I don't care what the devil says. If God says He will raise you up, it must be so. Forget everything else except what God says about Jesus."

A sixth time the power fell, and the sick man's lips began moving, and the tears began to fall. I said to him, "The power of God is here; it is yours to accept."

He said, "I have been bitter in my heart, and I know I have grieved the Spirit of God. Here I am, helpless. I cannot lift my hands or even lift a spoon to my mouth."

I said, "Repent, and God will hear you."

He repented and cried out, "O God, let this be to Your glory." As he said this, the power of the Lord went right through him.

I have asked the Lord never to let me tell this story except the way it happened, for I realize that God can never bless exaggerations. As we again said, "Jesus! Jesus! Jesus!" the bed shook, and the man shook.

I said to the people who were with me, "You can all go downstairs now. This is all God. I'm not going to assist him." I sat and watched that man get up and dress himself. We sang the doxology as he walked down the steps. I said to him, "Now, go tell what has happened."

The news soon spread everywhere that Lazarus had been raised up. People came from Llanelly and the surrounding district to see him and to hear his testimony. God brought salvation to many. Right out in the open air, this man told what God had done, and as a result, many were convicted and converted. All this occurred through the name of Jesus, *"through faith in His name"* (Acts 3:16). Yes, the faith that is by Him gave this sick man perfect soundness in the presence of them all.

A LAME MAN HEALED

In the passage from the third chapter of Acts, we read that Peter and John were helpless and uneducated. They had no college education. Nevertheless, they had been with Jesus. To them had come a wonderful revelation of the power of the name of Jesus. They had handed out the bread and fish after Jesus had multiplied them. They had sat at the table with Him, and John had often gazed into His face. Jesus often had had to rebuke Peter, but He had manifested His love to him through it all. Yes, He loved Peter, the wayward one.

Oh, He's a loving Savior! I have been wayward and stubborn. I had an unmanageable temper at one time, but how patient He has been. I am here to tell you that there is power in Jesus and in His wondrous name to transform anyone, to heal anyone.

If only you will see Him as God's Lamb, as God's beloved Son, upon whom was laid *"the iniquity of us all"* (Isaiah 53:6). If only you will see that Jesus paid the whole price for our redemption so that we might be free. Then you can enter into your purchased inheritance of salvation, of life, and of power.

Poor Peter and John! They had no money. But they had faith; they had the power of the Holy Spirit; they had God. You can have God even though you have nothing else. Even if you have lost your character, you can have God. I have seen the worst men saved by the power of God.

DEALING WITH A POTENTIAL MURDERER

I was preaching one day about the name of Jesus, and there was a man leaning against a lamppost, listening. He needed the lamppost to enable him to stay on his feet. We had finished our open-air meeting, and the man was still leaning against the lamppost. I asked him, "Are you sick?" He showed me his hand, and I saw that he held a silver-handled dagger inside his coat. He told me that he had been on his way to kill his unfaithful wife, but that he had heard me speaking about the power of the name of Jesus and could not get away. He said that he felt just helpless. I said, "Kneel down." There on the square, with people passing back and forth, he got saved.

I took him to my home and clothed him with a new suit. I saw that there was something in that man that God could use. He said to me the next morning, "God has revealed Jesus to me. I see that all has been laid upon Jesus." I lent him some money, and he soon got together a wonderful little home. His faithless wife was living with another man, but he invited her back to the home that he had prepared for her. She came. Where enmity and hatred had been before, the whole situation was transformed by love. God made that man a minister wherever he went.

Everywhere there is power in the name of Jesus. God can *"save to the uttermost"* (Hebrews 7:25).

AN "INCURABLE" MAN HEALED

There comes to mind a meeting we had in Stockholm that I will always remember. There was a home for incurables there, and one of the patients was brought to the meeting. He had palsy and was shaking all over. He stood up in front of three thousand people and came to the platform, supported by two others. The power of God fell on him as I anointed him in the name of Jesus. The moment I touched him, he dropped his crutches and began to walk in the name of Jesus. He walked down the steps and around that great building in view of all the people. There is nothing that our God cannot do. He will do everything if you will dare to believe.

Someone said to me, "Will you go to this home for incurables?" They took me there on my rest day. They brought out the sick people into a great corridor, and in one hour the Lord set about twenty of them free.

The name of Jesus is so marvelous. Peter and John had no conception of all that was in that name; neither had the man who had been lame from his mother's womb, who was laid daily at the gate. But they had faith to say, *"In the name of Jesus Christ of Nazareth, rise up and walk"* (Acts 3:6). And as Peter *"took him by the right hand and lifted him up,…immediately his feet and ankle bones received strength"* (verse 7), and he went into the temple with them, walking and leaping and praising God. God wants you to see more of this sort of thing done. How can it be done? Through *"His name, through faith in His name"* (verse 16); through faith that is by Him.

REVIVALS IN SCANDINAVIA

By Anna Lewini

The writer had the privilege for three months one year of being in the center of Mr. Smith Wigglesworth's meetings in both Sweden and Denmark. It was a time of visitation from on high. I estimate that hundreds of people received Jesus as their Savior; thousands were healed from all kinds of diseases; also thousands of believers awoke to a new kind of life; and many, many received the baptism of the Holy Spirit as on the Day of Pentecost. For all this we give glory to Jesus. Here are a few examples of miracles my eyes have seen.

It was in Orebro, Sweden, where at that time there was held a Pentecostal Convention. I came to seek help myself, being worn out with long, unbroken service in the Lord's work. The next day there was a meeting for healing. After the preaching service, I went forward into the other hall, and I was surprised to find a crowd following in a few minutes. The hall was soon full with hundreds of men and women patiently waiting for a touch from God through His servant. Glory to God, we were not disappointed. As hands were laid upon me, the power of God went through me in a mighty way. I was immediately well.

It was wonderful to notice, as the ministry continued, the effect upon the people as the power of God came over them. Some lifted their hands, crying, "I am healed! I am healed!"

Some fell on the platform under the power of the Spirit, having to be helped down. Others walked away as in a
dream; others as if drunk with new wine, lost to everything
but God; but all had faces transfigured with the glory of the
Lord and magnifying Jesus. A young blind girl, as she was
ministered to, cried out, "Oh, how many windows there are
in this hall!" During the three weeks the meetings continued, the great chapel was crowded daily, multitudes being
healed, and many saved. The testimony meetings were wonderful. One said, "I was deaf, they prayed, and Jesus healed
me." Another, "I had consumption, and I am free." And so
on.

At Skofde, in the smaller hall, set apart for those seeking
the baptism of the Holy Spirit, I shall never forget the sight,
how the people with eyes closed and hearts uplifted to God
waited. Did the Holy Spirit fall on them? Of course, He
did. Here also many were healed. At another place there
was a young man whose body was spoiled because of sin,
but the Lord is merciful with sinners. He was anointed, and
when hands were laid on, the power of God went mightily
over him. He said, "I am healed," but being broken down
as a little child, confessing his sin; at the same moment the
Lord saved him. Glory to God! He went into the large hall
and testified to salvation and healing.

At Stockholm, long lines waited for hours to get in. The
hall held eighteen hundred people. At nearly every meeting,
crowds were unable to enter the building, but they waited
on, often hours and hours, for the chance, if any left the
building, to step into the place. Here was a man with two
crutches, his whole body shaking with palsy, as he was lifted
onto the platform. (Behind him five or six hundred more

were waiting for help.) This man was anointed and hands were laid on him in the name of Jesus. He was still shaking. Then he dropped one crutch, and after a short time the other one. His body was still shaking, but he took the first step out *in faith*. Would it be? He lifted one foot and then the other, walked around the platform. The onlookers rejoiced with him. Then he walked around the auditorium. Hallelujah!

During the meeting a woman began to shout and shout. The preacher told her to be quiet, but instead she jumped up on a chair, flourishing her arms about and crying, "I am healed! I am healed! I had cancer in my mouth, and I was unsaved; but during the meeting, as I listened to the Word of God, the Lord saved me and healed me of cancer in my mouth." She shouted again, "I am saved! I am healed of cancer!" She was quite beside herself. The people laughed and cried together.

Here was another woman unable to walk, sitting in a chair as she was ministered to. Her experience was the same as hundreds of others. She rose up, looking around and wondering if, after all, it was a dream. Suddenly she laughed and said, "My leg is healed." Afterward, she said, "I am not saved," and streams of tears ran down her face. They prayed for her, and later she left the meeting, healed and saved and full of joy. We have a wonderful Savior. Glory to His holy name!

Out of many miracles in Norway, I quote two taken from Pastor Barratt's paper, *Korsets Seir* (The Victory of the Cross). A man and his son came in a taxi to the meeting. Both had crutches. The father had been in bed for two years and was unable to put his leg on the ground. He was ministered to first. He dropped both crutches, walking and praising God. When the son saw this, he cried out, "Help me, too," and after a little while the father and the son, without crutches and without a taxi, walked away from the hall together. The Word again is manifested; the same Jesus, the wonder-working Jesus, is just the same today.

Now Copenhagen, my homeland! During three weeks, thousands daily attended the meetings. Each morning two or three hundred were ministered to for healing. Each evening the platform was surrounded. Again and again, as each throng retired, another company came forward seeking salvation. Here many were baptized in the Holy Spirit. The testimony meetings were wonderful.

Now I will close with a vision given to a brother who attended these meetings. He was lost in intercession for the hundreds of sick waiting to be ministered to for healing. He saw an opening from the platform, where the sick were, right into glory. He saw wonderful beings in the form of men resting, who looked on with interest. Again he looked at the platform and saw a heavenly Being clothed in white, who all the time was more active than any other in helping the sick, and when *He* touched them, the effect was wonderful. Bent forms were made straight, their eyes shone, and they began to glorify and praise the Lord. A Voice said, "Healings are the smallest of the gifts; it is but a drop in the bucket in view of what God has in store for His children. You shall do greater works than these."

—from *Confidence*

26

Our Risen Christ

Now as they spoke to the people, the priests, the captain of the temple, and the Sadducees came upon them, being greatly disturbed that they taught the people and preached in Jesus the resurrection from the dead. And they laid hands on them, and put them in custody until the next day, for it was already evening. However, many of those who heard the word believed; and the number of the men came to be about five thousand.

And it came to pass, on the next day, that their rulers, elders, and scribes, as well as Annas the high priest, Caiaphas, John, and Alexander, and as many as were of the family of the high priest, were gathered together at Jerusalem. And when they had set them in the midst, they asked, "By what power or by what name have you done this?" Then Peter, filled with the Holy Spirit, said to them, "Rulers of the people and elders of Israel: If we this day are judged for a good deed done to a helpless man, by

*what means he has been made well, let it be known to you all,
and to all the people of Israel, that by the name of Jesus Christ
of Nazareth, whom you crucified, whom God raised from the
dead, by Him this man stands here before you whole. This is the
'stone which was rejected by you builders, which has become the
chief cornerstone.' Nor is there salvation in any other, for there
is no other name under heaven given among men by which we
must be saved."*

*Now when they saw the boldness of Peter and John, and per-
ceived that they were uneducated and untrained men, they marveled. And they realized that they had been with Jesus. And
seeing the man who had been healed standing with them, they
could say nothing against it. But when they had commanded
them to go aside out of the council, they conferred among themselves, saying, "What shall we do to these men? For, indeed,
that a notable miracle has been done through them is evident to
all who dwell in Jerusalem, and we cannot deny it. But so that
it spreads no further among the people, let us severely threaten
them, that from now on they speak to no man in this name."*

*So they called them and commanded them not to speak at all
nor teach in the name of Jesus. But Peter and John answered
and said to them, "Whether it is right in the sight of God to
listen to you more than to God, you judge. For we cannot but
speak the things which we have seen and heard." So when they
had further threatened them, they let them go, finding no way
of punishing them, because of the people, since they all glorified
God for what had been done. For the man was over forty years
old on whom this miracle of healing had been performed.*

*And being let go, they went to their own companions and re-
ported all that the chief priests and elders had said to them. So*

when they heard that, they raised their voice to God with one accord and said: "Lord, You are God, who made heaven and earth and the sea, and all that is in them, who by the mouth of Your servant David have said: 'Why did the nations rage, and the people plot vain things? The kings of the earth took their stand, and the rulers were gathered together against the LORD and against His Christ.' For truly against Your holy Servant Jesus, whom You anointed, both Herod and Pontius Pilate, with the Gentiles and the people of Israel, were gathered together to do whatever Your hand and Your purpose determined before to be done. Now, Lord, look on their threats, and grant to Your servants that with all boldness they may speak Your word, by stretching out Your hand to heal, and that signs and wonders may be done through the name of Your holy Servant Jesus." And when they had prayed, the place where they were assembled to-gether was shaken; and they were all filled with the Holy Spirit, and they spoke the word of God with boldness.

Now the multitude of those who believed were of one heart and one soul; neither did anyone say that any of the things he pos-sessed was his own, but they had all things in common. And with great power the apostles gave witness to the resurrection of the Lord Jesus. And great grace was upon them all. Nor was there anyone among them who lacked; for all who were posses-sors of lands or houses sold them, and brought the proceeds of the things that were sold, and laid them at the apostles' feet; and they distributed to each as anyone had need. And Joses, who was also named Barnabas by the apostles (which is translated Son of Encouragement), a Levite of the country of Cyprus, having land, sold it, and brought the money and laid it at the apostles' feet. (Acts 4)

We praise God that our glorious Jesus is the risen Christ. Those of us who have tasted the power of the indwelling Spirit know something about how the hearts of those two disciples burned as they walked to Emmaus with the risen Lord as their companion. (See Luke 24:13–31.)

Note the words of Acts 4:31: *"And when they had prayed, the place where they were assembled together was shaken."* There are many churches where they never pray the kind of prayer that you read of here. A church that does not know how to pray and to shout will never be shaken. If you live or worship in a place like that, you might as well write over the threshold: *"Ichabod…'The glory has departed from Israel!'"* (1 Samuel 4:21). It is only when men have learned the secret of prayer, power, and praise that God comes forth. Some people say, "Well, I praise God inwardly," but if there is an abundance of praise in your heart, your mouth cannot help speaking it.

WHAT IS INSIDE WILL COME OUT

A man who had a large business in London was a great church-goer. The church he attended was beautifully decorated, and his pew was delightfully cushioned—just enough to make it easy to sleep through the sermons. He was a prosperous man in business, but he had no peace in his heart. There was a boy at his business who always looked happy. He was always jumping and whistling. One day he said to this boy, "I want to see you in my office."

When the boy came to his office, the man asked him, "How is it that you can always whistle and be happy?"

"I cannot help it," answered the boy.

"Where did you get this happiness?" asked the gentleman.

"I got it at the Pentecostal mission."

"Where is that?" The boy told him, and the man began attending. The Lord reached his heart, and in a short while, he was entirely changed. One day, shortly after this, he found that instead of being distracted by his business as he formerly had been, he was actually whistling and jumping. His disposition and his whole life had been changed.

The shout cannot come out unless it is within. The inner working of the power of God must come first. It is He who changes the heart and transforms the life. Before there is any real outward evidence, there must be the inflow of divine life.

Sometimes I say to people, "You weren't at the meeting the other night."

They reply, "Oh, yes, I was there in spirit."

I say to them, "Well, next time come with your body also. We don't want a lot of spirits here and no bodies. We want you to come and get filled with God."

When all the people come and pray and praise as did these early disciples, there will be something happening. People who come will catch fire, and they will want to come again; but they will have no use for a place where everything has become formal, dry, and dead.

The power of Pentecost came to loose men. God wants us to be free. Men and women are tired of imitations; they want reality; they want to see people who have the living Christ within, who are filled with Holy Spirit power.

GOD IS ALWAYS ON TIME

I received several letters and telegrams about a certain case, but when I arrived, I was told I was too late. I said, "That cannot be. God has never sent me anywhere too late." God showed me that something different would happen than anything I had ever seen before. The people I went to were all strangers.

I was introduced to a young man who lay helpless, and for whom there was no hope. The doctor had been to see him that morning and had declared that he would not live through the day. He lay with his face to the wall, and when I spoke to him, he whispered, "I cannot turn over." His mother said that they had had to lift him out of bed on sheets for weeks, and that he was so frail and helpless that he had to stay in one position.

The young man said, "My heart is very weak." I assured him, "'*God is the strength of* [your] *heart and* [your] *portion forever*' (Psalm 73:26). If you will believe God, it will be so today."

Our Christ is risen. He is a living Christ who lives within us. We must not have this truth merely as a theory. Christ must be risen in us by the power of the Spirit. The power that raised Him from the dead must animate us, and as this glorious resurrection power surges through our beings, we will be freed from all our weaknesses. We will *"be strong in the Lord and in the power of His might"* (Ephesians 6:10). There is a resurrection power that God wants you to have and to have today. Why not receive your portion here and now?

I said to these people, "I believe your son will rise today." They only laughed. People do not expect to see signs and wonders today as the disciples saw them of old. Has God changed, or has our faith diminished so that we are not expecting the greater works that Jesus promised? We must not sing in any minor key. Our message must rise to concert pitch, and there must be nothing left out that is in the Book.

It was wintertime, and I said to the parents, "Will you get the boy's suit and bring it here?" They would not listen to the request, because they were expecting the boy to die. But I had gone to that place believing God.

We read about Abraham:

(As it is written, "I have made you a father of many nations")
in the presence of Him whom he believed; God...gives life to the
dead and calls those things which do not exist as though they
did. (Romans 4:17)

May God help us to understand this. It is time people knew how to shout in faith as they contemplate the eternal power of our God, to whom it is nothing to *"give life to your mortal bodies"* (Romans 8:11) and raise the dead. I come across some who would be giants in the power of God, but they have no shout of faith. Everywhere, I find people who become discouraged even when they are praying simply because they are just breathing sentences without uttering speech. You cannot win the victory that way. You must learn to take the victory and shout in the face of the devil, "It is done!"

There is no man who can doubt if he learns to shout. When we know how to shout properly, things will be different, and tremendous things will happen. In Acts 4:24 we read, *"They raised their voice to God with one accord."* It surely must have been a loud prayer. We must know that God means for us to have life. If there is anything in the world that has life in it, it is this Pentecostal revival we are in. I believe in the baptism of the Holy Spirit with the speaking in tongues, and I believe that every man who is baptized in the Holy

Spirit will *"speak with other tongues, as the Spirit* [gives him] *utterance"* (Acts 2:4). I believe in the Holy Spirit. And if you are filled with the Spirit, you will be superabounding in life, and living waters will flow from you.

At last I persuaded the parents to bring the boy's clothes and lay them on the bed. From the human viewpoint, the young man lay dying. I spoke to the afflicted lad, "God has revealed to me that as I lay my hands on you, the place will be filled with the Holy Spirit, the bed will be shaken, you will be shaken and thrown out of bed by the power of the Holy Spirit, and you will dress yourself and be strong." I said this to him in faith. I laid hands on him in the name of Jesus, and instantly the power of God fell and filled the place. I felt helpless and fell flat on the floor. I knew nothing except that a short while after the place was shaken.

Then I heard the young man walking over me and saying, "For Your glory, Lord! For Your glory, Lord!"

He dressed himself and cried, "God has healed me." The father fell, the mother fell, and another who was present also fell. God manifested His power that day in saving the whole household and healing the young man. It is the power of the risen Christ we need. Today, that young man is preaching the Gospel.

GOD IS AT WORK

For years we have been longing for God to come forth, and, praise Him, He is coming forth. The tide is rising everywhere. I was in Switzerland not long ago, preaching in many places where the Pentecostal message had not been heard. Today, there are nine new Pentecostal assemblies in different places going on blessedly for God. All over the world it is the same; this great Pentecostal work is in motion. You can hardly go to a place now where God is not pouring out His Spirit upon hungry hearts. God has promised to pour out His Spirit upon all flesh, and His promises never fail. Our Christ is risen. His salvation was not a thing done in a corner. Truly He was a man of glory who went to Calvary for us in order that He might free us from all that would mar and hinder, that He might transform us by His grace and bring us out from under the power of the enemy into the glorious power of God. One touch of our risen Christ will raise the dead. Hallelujah!

Oh, this wonderful Jesus of ours comes and indwells us! He comes to abide. It is He who baptizes us with the Holy Spirit and makes everything different. We are to be a *"kind of firstfruits"* (James 1:18) unto God and are to be like Christ who is the First Fruit. We are to walk in His footsteps and live in His power. What a salvation this is, having this risen Christ in us. I feel that everything else must go to nothingness, helplessness, and ruin. Even the best thought of holiness must be on the decrease in order that Christ may increase. All things are under the power of the Spirit.

GOD IS WITH YOU

Dare you take your inheritance from God? Dare you believe God? Dare you stand on the record of His Word? What is the record? If you will believe, you will see the glory of God. (See John 11:40.) You will be sifted as wheat. You will be tested as though some strange thing tried you. (See 1 Peter 4:12.) You will be put in places where you will have to put your whole trust in God. There is no such thing as anyone being tested beyond what God will allow. There is no temptation that will come, but God will be with you right in the temptation to deliver you (see 1 Corinthians 10:13), and when you have been tried, He will bring you forth as gold. (See Job

23:10.) Every trial is to bring you to a greater position in God. The trial that tries your faith will take you on to the place where you will know that the faith of God will be forthcoming in the next test. No man is able to win any victory except through the power of the risen Christ within him. You will never be able to say, "I did this or that." You will desire to give God the glory for everything.

If you are sure of your ground, if you are counting on the presence of the living Christ within, you can laugh when you see things getting worse. God wants you to be settled and grounded in Christ, and it is only as you are filled with the Holy Spirit that you become steadfast and unmovable in Him.

The Lord Jesus said, "*I have a baptism to be baptized with, and how distressed I am till it is accomplished!*" (Luke 12:50). Assuredly, He was distressed all along the way: in Gethsemane, in the judgment hall, and, after that, on the cross, where He, "*through the eternal Spirit offered Himself without spot to God*" (Hebrews 9:14). God will take us right on in like manner, and the Holy Spirit will lead every step of the way. God led Him right through to the empty tomb, to the glory of the Ascension, to a place on the throne. The Son of God will never be satisfied until He has us with Himself, sharing His glory and sharing His throne.

27

Gifts of Healing and the Working of Miracles

To another [are given] the gifts of healing by the same Spirit; to another the working of miracles. (1 Corinthians 12:9–10 KJV)

God has given us much in these last days, and where much is given, much will be required. (See Luke 12:48.) The Lord has said to us:

You are the salt of the earth; but if the salt loses its flavor, how shall it be seasoned? It is then good for nothing but to be thrown out and trampled underfoot by men. (Matthew 5:13)

Our Lord Jesus expressed a similar thought when He said, *"If anyone does not abide in Me, he is cast out as a branch and is withered;*

and they gather them and throw them into the fire, and they are burned" (John 15:6). On the other hand, He told us, *"If you abide in Me, and My words abide in you, you will ask what you desire, and it shall be done for you"* (John 15:7).

If we do not move on with the Lord in these days, and if we do not walk in the light of revealed truth, we will become as flavorless salt or a withered branch. This one thing we must do: *"Forgetting those things which are behind"*—both the past failures and the past blessings—we must reach forth for those things that are before us and *"press toward the mark for the prize of the high calling of God in Christ Jesus"* (Philippians 3:13–14 KJV).

For many years, the Lord has been moving me on and keeping me from spiritual stagnation. When I was in the Wesleyan Methodist Church, I was sure I was saved, and I was sure I was all right. The Lord said to me, "Come out," and I came out. When I was with the people known as the Brethren, I was sure I was all right then. But the Lord said, "Come out." Then I went into the Salvation Army. At that time, it was full of life, and there were revivals everywhere. But the Salvation Army went into natural things, and the great revivals that they had in those early days ceased. The Lord said to me, "Come out," and I came out. I have had to come out three times since.

I believe that this Pentecostal revival that we are now in is the best thing that the Lord has on the earth today; and yet I believe that God will bring something out of this revival that is going to be still better. God has no use for anyone who is not hungering and thirsting for even more of Himself and His righteousness.

The Lord has told us to *"earnestly desire the best gifts"* (1 Corinthians 12:31), and we need to earnestly desire those gifts that will bring Him the most glory. We need to see the gifts of heal-ing and the working of miracles in operation today. Some say it is necessary for us to have the gift of discernment in operation with the gifts of healing, but even apart from this gift, I believe that the Holy Spirit will have a divine revelation for us as we deal with the sick.

Most people think they have discernment; but if they would turn their discernment on themselves for twelve months, they would never want to "discern" again. The gift of discernment is not criticism. I am satisfied that in Pentecostal circles today, our para-mount need is more perfect love.

Perfect love will never want the preeminence in every-thing; it will never want to take the place of another; it will always be willing to take the back seat. If you go to a Bible conference, there is always someone who wants to give a message, who wants to be heard. If you have a desire to go to a conference, you should have three things settled in your mind: Do I want to be heard? Do I want to be seen? Do I want anything on the line of finances? If I have these things in my heart, I have no right to be there.

The one thing that must move us is the constraining love of God to minister for Him. A preacher always loses out when he gets his mind on finances. It is advisable for Pentecostal preachers to avoid making much of finances except to stir people up to help support our missionaries financially. A preacher who gets big collections for the missionaries never needs to fear; the Lord will take care of his finances.

A preacher should not arrive at a place and say that God has sent him. I am always fearful when I hear a man advertising this. If he is sent by God, the believers will know it. God has His plans for

His servants, and we must live in His plans so completely that He will place us where He wants us. If you seek nothing but the will of God, He will always put you in the right place at the right time.

I want you to see that the gifts of healing and the working of miracles are part of the Spirit's plan and will come forth in operation as we are working along that plan. I must know the movement of the Spirit and the voice of God. I must understand the will of God if I am to see the gifts of the Spirit in operation.

MINISTERING HEALING

The gifts of healing are so varied. You may go to see ten people, and every case will be different. I am never happier in the Lord than when I am in a bedroom with a sick person. I have had more revelations of the Lord's presence when I have ministered to the sick at their bedsides than at any other time. It is as your heart goes out to the needy ones in deep compassion that the Lord manifests His presence. You are able to discern their conditions. It is then that you know you must be filled with the Spirit to deal with the conditions before you.

When people are sick, you frequently find that they are ignorant about Scripture. They usually know three Scriptures, though. They know about Paul's *"thorn in the flesh"* (2 Corinthians 12:7); they know that Paul told Timothy to take *"a little wine"* for his *"stomach's sake"* (1 Timothy 5:23); and they know that Paul left someone sick somewhere, but they don't remember his name or the place, and they don't know in what chapter of the Bible it is found. (See 2 Timothy 4:20.) Most people think they have a thorn in the flesh. The chief thing in dealing with a person who is sick is to discern his exact condition. As you are ministering under the Spirit's power, the

Lord will let you see just what will be the most helpful and the most faithinspiring to him.

When I was in the plumbing business, I enjoyed praying for the sick. Urgent calls would come, and I would have no time to wash. With my hands all black, I would preach to these sick ones, my heart all aglow with love. Ah, your heart must be in it when you pray for the sick. You have to get right to the bottom of the cancer with a divine compassion, and then you will see the gifts of the Spirit in operation.

I was called at ten o'clock one night to pray for a young person who was dying of consumption and whom the doctor had given up for dead. As I looked, I saw that unless God intervened, it would be impossible for her to live.

I turned to the mother and said, "Well, Mother, you will have to go to bed."

She said, "Oh, I have not had my clothes off for three weeks."

I said to the daughters, "You will have to go to bed," but they did not want to go. It was the same with the son.

I put on my overcoat and said, "Good-bye, I'm leaving."

They said, "Oh, don't leave us."

I said, "I can do nothing here."

They said, "Oh, if you will stay, we will all go to bed."

I knew that God would not move in an atmosphere of mere natural sympathy and unbelief. They all went to bed, and I stayed, and that was surely a time as I knelt by that bed face-to-face with death

242 Best of Smith Wigglesworth

and the devil. But God can change the hardest situation and make you know that He is almighty.

Then the fight came. It seemed as though the heavens were brass. I prayed from 11:00 p.m. to 3:30 a.m. I saw the glimmering light on the face of the sufferer and saw her pass away. Satan said, "Now you are done for. You have come from Bradford, and the girl has died on your hands."

I said, "It can't be. God did not send me here for nothing. This is a time to change strength." I remembered the passage that said, *"Men always ought to pray and not lose heart"* (Luke 18:1). Death had taken place, but I knew that God was all-powerful and that He who had split the Red Sea is just the same today. It was a time when I would not accept "No" and God said "Yes."

I looked at the window, and at that moment, the face of Jesus appeared. It seemed as though a million rays of light were coming from His face. As He looked at the one who had just passed away, the color came back to her face. She rolled over and fell asleep. Then I had a glorious time. In the morning she woke early, put on a dressing gown, and walked to the piano. She started to play and to sing a wonderful song. The mother and the sister and the brother all came down to listen. The Lord had intervened. A miracle had been worked.

The Lord is calling us along this way. I thank God for difficult cases. The Lord has called us into heart union with Himself; He wants His bride to have one heart and one Spirit with Him and to do what He Himself loved to do. That case had to be a miracle. The lungs were gone; they were just in shreds. Yet the Lord restored her lungs, making them perfectly sound.

A fruit of the Spirit that must accompany the gift of healing is long-suffering. The man who is persevering with God to be used in healing must be a man of long-suffering. He must always be ready with a word of comfort. If the sick one is in distress and helpless and does not see everything eye-to-eye with you, you must bear with him. Our Lord Jesus Christ was filled with compassion and lived and moved in a place of long-suffering, and we will have to get into this place if we are to help needy ones.

There are times when you pray for the sick, and you seem to be rough with them. But you are not dealing with a person; you are dealing with satanic forces that are binding the person. Your heart is full of love and compassion toward all; however, you are moved to a holy anger as you see the place the devil has taken in the body of the sick one, and you deal with his position with a real forcefulness.

One day a pet dog followed a lady out of her house and ran all around her feet. She said to the dog, "My dear, I cannot have you with me today." The dog wagged its tail and made a big fuss. She said, "Go home, my dear." But the dog did not go. At last she shouted roughly, "Go home," and off it went. Some people deal with the devil like that. Satan can stand all the comfort you like to give him. Cast him out! You are not dealing with the person; you are dealing with the devil. Demon power must be dislodged in the name of the Lord.

You are always right when you dare to deal with sickness as with the devil. Much sickness is caused by some misconduct; there is something wrong, there is some neglect somewhere, and the enemy has had a chance to get in. It is necessary to repent and confess where you have given place to the devil (see Ephesians 4:27), and then he can be dealt with.

When you deal with a cancer case, recognize that a living evil spirit is destroying the body. I had to pray for a woman in Los Angeles one time who was suffering with a cancerous growth, and as soon as the cancer was cursed, it stopped bleeding. It was dead. The next thing that happened was that the natural body pushed it out, because the natural body had no room for dead matter. It came out like a great big ball with tens of thousands of fibers. All these fibers had been pressing into the flesh. These evil powers move to get further hold of the body's system, but the moment they are destroyed, their hold is gone. Jesus told His disciples that He gave them power to loose and power to bind. (See Matthew 16:19.) It is our privilege in the power of the Holy Spirit to loose the prisoners of the enemy and to let the oppressed go free.

Take your position from the first epistle of John and declare, *"He who is in* [me] *is greater than he who is in the world"* (1 John 4:4). Then recognize that it is not you who has to deal with the power of the devil, but the Greater One who is within you. Oh, what it means to be filled with Him! You can do nothing in yourself, but He who is in you will win the victory. Your being has become the temple of the Holy Spirit. Your mouth, your mind, your whole being may be used and worked upon by the Spirit of God.

I was called to a certain town in Norway. The hall seated about fifteen hundred people. When I got to the place, it was packed, and hundreds were trying to get in. There were some policemen there. The first thing I did was to preach to the people outside the building. Then I said to the policemen, "It hurts me very much that there are more people outside than inside, and I feel I must preach to the people. I would like you to get me the marketplace to preach in." They secured a large park for me, and a big stand was erected, and I was able to preach to thousands.

After the preaching, we had some marvelous cases of healing. One man came a hundred miles, bringing his food with him. He had not been passing anything through his stomach for over a month because he had a large cancer on his stomach. He was healed at that meeting, and opening his package, he began eating for all the people to see.

There was a young woman there with a stiff hand. When she was a child, her mother, instead of making her use her arm, had allowed her to keep it dormant until it was stiff. This young woman was like the woman in the Bible who was bent over with the spirit of infirmity. (See Luke 13:11.) As she stood before me, I cursed the spirit of infirmity in the name of Jesus. It was instantly cast out, and the arm was free. Then she waved her hand all around.

At the close of the meeting, the devil threw two people to the ground with fits. When the devil is manifesting himself, then is the time to deal with him. Both of these people were delivered, and when they stood up and thanked and praised the Lord, what a wonderful time we had.

We need to wake up and strive to believe God. Before God could bring me to this place, He broke me a thousand times. I have wept; I have groaned. I have travailed many a night until God broke me. It seems to me that until God has mowed you down, you can never have this long-suffering, this endurance, for others. We will never have the gifts of healing and the working of miracles in operation unless we stand in the divine power that God gives us, unless we stand believing God and *"having done all"* (Ephesians 6:13), we still stand believing.

We have been seeing wonderful miracles during these last days, and they are only a little of what we are going to see. I believe that we are right on the threshold of wonderful things, but I want to emphasize that all these things will be only through the power of the Holy Spirit. You must not think that these gifts will fall upon you like ripe cherries. There is a sense in which you have to pay the price for everything you get. We must earnestly desire God's best gifts and say "Amen" to any preparation the Lord takes us through. In this way, we will be humble, useable vessels through whom He Himself can operate by means of the Spirit's power.

Smith Wigglesworth on Heaven

28

Life Everlasting

You may be amazed, when you step into the heavenly glory, to find there the very Word, the very life, the very touch that has caused aspiration and inspiration. The Word is settled there. The Word creates right in our very nature this wonderful touch of divine inspiration, making us know that those who are in heaven and we who are on earth are of one spirit, blended in one harmonious knowledge, created in a new order. We are being made like Him by the power of the spirit of the Word of God, until we are full of hopefulness, filled with life, joyously expecting, gloriously waiting.

One word is continually sufficient for me:

Therefore, having been justified by faith, we have peace with God through our Lord Jesus Christ, through whom also we have access by faith into this grace in which we stand, and rejoice in hope of the glory of God. (Romans 5:1–2)

Salvation fills us with the *"hope of the glory of God,"* with a great access into the grace.

Let us turn to the sixth chapter of John. We are still on the foundation of the construction of the saint of God in the new order of the Spirit. We are still building upon the foundation principles of the living Word of God, not so that we may be like those who are drunk in the night, or those who are asleep, but so that we will be awakened. (See 1 Thessalonians 5:5–8.)

Being awakened does not mean particularly that you have been actually asleep; the word *sleeping* in this context doesn't mean a person is actually asleep. It means that he is dense to activity relating to the spiritual realm. Sleeping does not mean that you are fast asleep. Sleeping means that you have lost understanding, you are dull of hearing, and your eyes are heavy because they are not full of the light that will light you. So God is causing us to understand that we have to be alive and awake.

Here is the word: *"Do not labor for the food which perishes"* (John 6:27). At the beginning of John 6, Jesus had been feeding the sheep, and because they were being fed by His gracious hands, the crowd came around Him again. He saw that they were of the natural order, and He broke forth into this wonderful word, *"Do not labor for the food which perishes."*

INTERPRETATION OF TONGUES

The Lord Jesus, seeing the needy missing the great ideal of His mission, turned their attention by saying, "It is more needful that you get a drink of a spiritual awakening. It is more needful that you eat of the inner manna of Christ today, for God has sealed Him for that purpose and He has become the Bread for you."

The Master was in earnest when He said, *"Enter by the narrow gate; for wide is the gate and broad is the way that leads to destruction"* (Matthew 7:13).

Strive to enter in at the narrow gate. Get a live, inward inheritance in you. See that the Master has food for us, bread enough and to spare.

INTERPRETATION OF TONGUES

It is the living Word. It is the touch of His own spiritual nature that He wants to breathe into our human nature today. It is the nature of the Son; it is the breath of His life; it is the quickening of His power; it is the savor of life unto life. It is that which quickens you from death into life; it is that which wakens you out of all human into the glorious liberty of the sons of God. It is the Spirit that quickens.

Let me read the Word:

Do not labor for the food which perishes, but for the food which endures to everlasting life, which the Son of Man will give you, because God the Father has set His seal on Him. (John 6:27)

Everlasting life is a gift. The Holy Spirit is a gift. But *"the gift of God is eternal life"* (Romans 6:23), and we have this life in His Son. (See 1 John 5:11.) *"He who does not have the Son of God does not have life"* (verse 12), but he who has the Son *"has passed from death into life"* (John 5:24). This is the life that will be caught up; this is the life that will be changed in a moment; this is the life that will enter into the presence of God in a moment of time, because it is divine, because it has no bondage, because it is not hindered by the flesh.

THE BEGINNING OF LIFE

So God is pruning us, teaching us to observe that those who enter into this life have ceased from their own works. (See Hebrews 4:10.) Those who enter into this spiritual awakening have no more bondages. They have learned that *"no one engaged in warfare entangles himself with the affairs of this life"* (2 Timothy 2:4). They have a new inspiration of divine power. It is the nature of the Son of God.

But the verse says, *"Strive to enter through the narrow gate"* (Luke 13:24). Yes, beloved, this means you will have to work for it, because your own nature will interfere with you; your friends will often stand in the way. Your position will many times almost bring you to a place where you will be doomed if you take that stand.

I understand that Jesus could be interpreted in no other way but this: *"Whoever desires to save his life will lose it, but whoever loses his life for My sake will find it"* (Matthew 16:25). He will find the life that never ceases. Human life has an end; divine life has only a beginning. This is the life that the Son of Man was sealed to give. He was specially sealed; He was specially anointed; He was specially separated. He gave Himself over to God, so that He might become the firstfruit of the first-begotten of a new creation that was going to be in the presence of God forever. A new creation, a new sonship, a new adoption, a new place, a new power. Hallelujah! Are you in for it?

The apostle Peter had entered into this divine position just before Jesus made His statement, *"Whoever desires to save his life will lose it, but whoever loses his life for My sake will find it"* (Matthew

16:25). Peter had just gotten this new life; he had just entered into the place where he knew that Jesus was the Son of God, saying, *"You are the Christ, the Son of the living God"* (verse 16). Then Jesus began breaking the seal of His ministry. He said, *"The Son of Man must be delivered into the hands of sinful men, and be crucified, and the third day rise again"* (Luke 24:7).

Peter said, "This will not happen. I'll see to that! You leave that business with me. Let anybody touch you, and I will stand in your place; I will be with you." And Jesus said, *"Get behind Me, Satan! You are an offense to Me, for you are not mindful of the things of God, but the things of men"* (Matthew 16:23).

Anything that hinders me from falling into the ground, everything that interferes with my taking up my cross, dying to self, separating from the world, cleaning my life up, or entering through the narrow gate, anything that interferes with that is Satan's power. *"Unless a grain of wheat falls into the ground and dies, it remains alone"* (John 12:24).

Strive to enter in. Seek to be worthy to enter in. Let God be honored by your leaving behind the things that you know are taking your life, hindering your progress, blighting your prospects, and ruining your mind—for nothing will dull the mind's perceptions like touching earthly things that are not clean.

When God began dealing with me on holy lines, I was working for thirteen saloons, meaning that I was going to thirteen different bars. Of course, I was among hundreds of other customers. God dealt with me in this matter, and I cleared up the whole situation in the presence of God. That was only one thing; there were a thousand things.

God wants us to be holy, pure, and perfect the whole way through. The inheritance is an incorruptible inheritance; it is unde-filed, and it does not fade away. (See 1 Peter 1:4.) Those who are entering in are judging themselves so that they will not be condemned with the world. (See 1 Corinthians 11:32.) Many people have fallen asleep. (See verses 27–30.) Why? Because they did not listen to the correction of the Word of the Lord. Some have been ill, and God dealt with them; they would not heed, and then God put them to sleep.

Oh, that God the Holy Spirit will have a choice with us today, that we will judge ourselves so that we are not condemned with the world! *"For if we would judge ourselves, we would not be judged"* (verse 31). What is it to judge yourself? If the Lord speaks, if He says, "Let it go," no matter if it is as dear as your right eye, you must let it go. If it is as costly as your right foot, you must let it go. It is far better to let it go.

Strive to enter in.

INTERPRETATION OF TONGUES

God's Word never speaks in vain. It always opens to you the avenues where you can enter in. God opens the door for you. He speaks to your heart; He is dealing with you. We are dealing with the coming of the Lord, but how will we be prepared unless all is burned? The wood, the hay, the stubble must be burned. The gold, the silver, and the precious stones will be preserved.

Be willing, beloved, for the Lord Himself has to deal with you.

THE BREAD OF LIFE

Let us move on to another important lesson of Scripture:

Then Jesus said to them, "Most assuredly, I say to you, Moses did not give you the bread from heaven, but My Father gives you the true bread from heaven. For the bread of God is He who comes down from heaven and gives life to the world."
(John 6:32–33)

Bread! Oh, beloved, I want God to give you a spiritual appetite so that you will have a great inward devouring place where you will eat the Word, where you will savor it with joy, where you will have it with grace, and also where it will be mingled with separation. As the Word comes to you—the Word of God, the Bread of Heaven, the very thing you need, the very nature of the life of the Son of God—and as you eat, you will be made in a new order after Him who has created you for His plan and purpose.

"Then they said to Him, 'Lord, give us this bread always'" (verse 34). I want that same expression to be made in our hearts because He is helping us into this.

"And Jesus said to them, 'I am the bread of life. He who comes to Me shall never hunger, and he who believes in Me shall never thirst'" (John 6:35).

The process of the Word of God must kindle in us a separation from the world. It must bring death to everything except the life of the Word of Christ in our hearts. I want to save you from judging, because to the degree that you have not come into the revelation of this eternal working in you, to that degree you will not come right through believing in the true principle of the Word of Life.

"He who comes to Me shall never hunger, and he who believes in Me shall never thirst."

The two things are necessary. I will never expect any person to go beyond his light. The Word of God is to give you light. The Spirit of the Lord and the Word of the Lord—one is light, the other is life. We must see that God wants us to have these two divine properties, life and light, so that we are in a perfect place to judge ourselves by the Word of God. The Word of God will stand true, whatever our opinions may be. Scripture says very truly, *"For what if some did not believe? Will their unbelief make the faithfulness of God without effect?"* (Romans 3:3). Will it change the Word? The Word of God will be the same whether people believe it or not.

In these meetings, God will sift the believer. This is a sifting meeting. I want you to get away from the chaff. Chaff is judgment; chaff is unbelief; chaff is fear; chaff is failing. It is the covering of the weak, and as long as it covers the weak, it hinders the weak from coming forth for bread. So God has to deal with the chaff; He has to get it away so that you might be the pure bread, the pure life, the pure word, and so that there will be no strange thing in you, no misunderstanding.

God has to deal with His people, and if God deals with the house of God, then the world will soon be dealt with. The dealing first is with the house of God, and then after that with the world. (See 1 Peter 4:17.) When the house of God is right, all the people will get right very soon. The principle is this: all the world needs and longs to be right, and so we have to be salt and light to guide them, to lead them, to operate before them so that they see our good works and glorify our Lord.

I was preaching on these divine elements one day, and one person in the midst of the meeting said, "I won't believe! I won't believe! Nothing like that ever moves me. You cannot move me. Nothing can move me."

"I believe! I believe! I believe!" I responded.

I went on dealing with the things of God. This man was a well-known preacher. He had come to a place where the chaff had to be taken up, where God was dealing with him, where his life was opened out. He said again, "I won't believe!" It made no difference to me; I went on preaching. He was so aroused that he jumped up and went out, shouting as he closed the door, "I won't believe!"

The next morning, the pastor of the church at which the meeting was being held, got a note saying, "Please come immediately," and the pastor went. As soon as he got to the door, a woman met him, tears in her eyes, weeping bitterly.

"Oh," she said, "I am in great distress!"

She took him inside. When he got inside, the first thing that confronted him was the man who had shouted out, "I won't believe!" The man got a piece of paper and wrote, "Last night I had a chance to believe; I refused to believe, and now I cannot believe, and I cannot speak."

This man was made mute because he would not believe. Is he the only one? No. We read the story of Zacharias and Elizabeth. When Zacharias was in the Holy of Holies, God spoke to him, telling him that He was going to give him a son. But his heart was unmoved, and his language was contrary to faith; so Gabriel said to him, "You will be mute and not able to speak...because you did not believe" (Luke 1:20). And he came out of that place mute.

It seems to me that if we will not judge ourselves, we will be judged. (See 1 Corinthians 11:31.) I am giving you the Word. The Word should so be in you that, as I speak, the fire should burn, the life should be kindled, the very nature of Christ should transform you. You should be so moved in this meeting that you are ready for rapture, and longing for it. You know that you have the life, and you know this life will be held until it gets loose.

You need the Bread to feed the life to you. The Word of God is the Bread. There is no famine going on now; God is giving us the Bread of Life.

"He who comes to Me shall never hunger, and he who believes in Me shall never thirst" (John 6:35). It is a constant satisfaction, an inward joyful expression, a place of peace.

> *All that the Father gives Me will come to Me, and the one who comes to Me I will by no means cast out. For I have come down from heaven, not to do My own will, but the will of Him who sent Me. This is the will of the Father who sent Me, that of all He has given Me I should lose nothing, but should raise it up at the last day.* (verses 37–39)

Nothing—I will lose nothing! Do you believe that? Some people are still on the hedge, undecided. "After all, He may lose us." I would rather believe the Word of God!

ONLY BELIEVE

I find people continually deceived because they look around them, and many people have lost all because of their feelings. There was one man in the Old Testament who was very terribly deceived because of his feelings—it was Jacob. He felt for Esau, but he was deceived. If you feel, you will be deceived.

God does not want us to feel. He wants us on one line only: believing. I would like you to understand that you did not come to Jesus. God gave you to Jesus. Where did He find you? He found you in the world, and He gave you to Jesus, and Jesus gave you eternal life. As He received everyone whom He had given His life for and given His life to, He said He would lose nothing; He would preserve them.

"Oh," you say, "that all depends."

Yes, it does, it depends upon whether you believe God or not. But I find people always getting outside of the plan of God because they use their own judgment.

I am not going to believe that all who say they are believers, believe. There was one group who came up to Jesus and said, "We are the seed of Abraham; we have Abraham for our father." (See John 8:39.) He said, "You are mistaken; you are the seed of the devil." (See verses 39–44.)

"He who believes in the Son of God has the witness" (1 John 5:10), and we know that we are the sons of God because we do those things that please Him. We know we are the sons of God because we love to keep His commandments. *"His commandments are not grievous"* (1 John 5:3 KJV). And we know we are the sons of God because we overcome the world. (See verse 4.)

That is what every son of God has to do—overcome the world. And this life we receive from Him is eternal and everlasting and cannot see corruption. But God is feeding us this morning with that wonderful Word of promise, so that we might know that we have the inheritance in the Spirit, and so that we may know that we are going on to the place of "Ready, Lord, ready!"

Are you ready to go? I am here getting you ready to go, because you have to go. It is impossible for the life of God or the law of the life of the Spirit to be in you unless it is doing its work. The law of the life of the Spirit will be putting to death all the natural life and will quicken you continually with spiritual life until you will have to go.

When I see white hair and wrinkled faces, I say, "You have to go. It does not matter what you say, you cannot stop; you have to go. You will begin blossoming, and in a short time you will bloom and be off."

That is a natural plan, but I am talking about a supernatural plan. We know that as we have borne the image of the earthly, we are going to bear the image of the heavenly. (See 1 Corinthians 15:49.) Mortality will be swallowed up in life. The very nature of the Son of God is in us, making life, immortality, and power. The power of the Word of the living Christ!

The Gospel of the grace of God has power to bring immortality and life. What is the Gospel? The Word, the Bread of the Son of God. Feed upon it. Feed upon it in your heart. It is immortality; it is life by the Word of quickening and by the Word of truth.

You look good, you are an inspiration, but you know there are many marks and blemishes. You know that as you pass through the weary days of toil, battling with sin on every line, there is a light in you, a life in you that is going to pass off, and you are going to be like Him. It will be the same face, but the marks, the scars, and the spots will have gone. What will do it? The Bread! Oh, Lord, ever more give us this Bread, the Bread of the Son of God!

"Most assuredly, I say to you, he who believes in Me has everlasting life. I am the bread of life" (John 6:47–48). Everlasting life means Bread. Men cannot live by bread alone, but by the Word of the living God. (See Matthew 4:4.)

TRIED BY FIRE, ENRICHED BY GRACE

When I read this in the book of Revelation, my heart was moved: *"And His name is called The Word of God"* (Revelation 19:13). His name, the very name, is the Word of God, who gave His life for the world. And of His life, of His Spirit, of His grace, of His faith we have received. What does this mean? Oh, you tried ones, grace is being poured into you—grace from heaven, grace enriched, grace abundant. His grace is for your weakness, so that you might be sustained in the trial, in the fire, passing through it, coming out more like the Lord.

This inspires me. Why? Because time comes to an end. All the beautiful buildings in the world, the mountains, the heavens and all, will pass away. The heavens will be rolled up as a scroll (see Isaiah 34:4), and all things *"will melt with fervent heat"* (2 Peter 3:10). But one thing cannot be burned; one thing cannot be changed; one thing can stand the fire, the water, persecution, and anything else. What is it? The same thing that went into the fire and remained untouched while the men on the outside were slain by the fire.

Shadrach, Meshach, and Abednego were in the fire, and it did not burn them. The king was amazed when he saw them walking. "Oh!" he said. *"Did we not cast three men bound into the midst of the fire?"* (Daniel 3:24).

"True, O king" (verse 24), his men replied.

"'Look!' he answered, 'I see four men loose, walking in the midst of the fire…and the form of the fourth is like the Son of God'" (verse 25).

There is no consuming. There is a life of the Son of God that cannot be burned, cannot see corruption, passes through fire, passes through clouds, passes through legions of demons and will clear them out of the way, passes through everything. Oh, that life! What is it? The life of the Son of God. He came to give life; He came to give life more abundantly. Oh, what a life, abounding life, resurrection life!

Do you have it? Is it yours? Are you afraid you will lose it? Do you believe He will lose you?

"What makes you say that?" you ask.

Because sometimes I hear doubters. So I am going to read a wonderful Scripture for the doubters.

> *My sheep hear My voice, and I know them, and they follow Me. And I give them eternal life, and they shall never perish; neither shall anyone snatch them out of My hand. My Father, who has given them to Me, is greater than all; and no one is able to snatch them out of My Father's hand.* (John 10:27–29)

Oh, that life—full of deity, full of assurance, full of victory, full of a shout. There is the shout of a King in the midst of you this morning. Will you be ready? How can you help it? Is it possible not to be ready? Why, it is not your life, it is His life. You did not seek Him; it was He who sought you. You cannot keep yourself; it is He who keeps you. You did not make the offering; it was God who made the offering. So it is all of grace. But what a wonderful grace!

INTERPRETATION OF TONGUES

The trumpet will blow and all will be brought forth, for God will bring them with Him, and those who are awake will not interfere with those who are asleep, but all with one breath will rise. What will rise? The life will rise to meet the Life that has preserved it, and we will be ever with the Lord.

What is going? The life. He gives everlasting life, and they will never perish.

Oh, where is your faith? Is your faith inspired? Are you quickened? Is there within you a truth that is saying, "I feel it, I know it. It moves me; I have it"? Yes, and you will be there in heaven—as surely as you are here, you will be there.

This thing that we are entering into is going to continue forever. Let us feed on this Bread; let us live in this holy atmosphere. This is divine nature that God is causing us to know, which will last forever.

Keep us, Lord, in a place of buying up opportunities, burning up bridges, paying the prices, denying ourselves so that we might be worthy of being Your own forever.

QUESTIONS ANSWERED

Q: Is there distinction in the Word between the life that brings forth the Rapture and eternal life where some first go down into the grave?

A: No. Those asleep in Jesus have the same life, but they are not asleep in the grave. They fall asleep to rest, but it is not a sleep or a rest of the spirit. The spirit never sleeps; the soul never sleeps. Solomon wrote, "*I sleep, but my heart is awake*" (Song of Solomon 5:2). Remember that the moment the body is put to rest, the spirit requires no rest; it is always young, it will know nothing about time.

Whichever way the body goes, it will be the same. If it goes to the grave, what will happen? The body, all that is earthly, will pass away; it will come to dust. Suppose it goes up. The Word of God says it will be dissolved. The same thing, it will be dissolved either way it goes. Why? Because flesh and blood are not going there, but the life of the Son of God is. God will provide a new body, resembling the old in every way—likeness, character, everything. The human spirit will enter into a celestial body whether it goes up or down—only we want you all to go up.

Q: I have heard Revelation 3:5 brought up to prove that a name could be blotted out of the Book of Life. Will you please explain?

A: I am dealing with people who are receiving everlasting life, who are not going to be lost. I am persuaded of better things than that of you. I will never believe that any human being is greater than my God. I believe that God is greater than all and that God can preserve us all. But I do believe that there are any number of people who have tried to make people believe they are the seed of God when they have not really been born again.

The life of the new birth is always seeking after God; it has no time for falling away from God, no time for the world; it is always hungry for God. Unless you get this fundamental truth deep down in your heart, you will fail, because you have to go on to holiness, inseparableness. *"Holiness adorns Your house, O Lord"* (Psalm 93:5). How can you be anything but holy and long to be holy?

29

The Appointed Hour: Life out of Death

The communion service is a very blessed time for us to gather together in remembrance of the Lord. I want to remind you of this fact, that this is the only service we render to the Lord. All other services we attend are for us to get a blessing from the Lord, but Jesus said, *"Do this in remembrance of Me"* (Luke 22:19). We have gathered together to commemorate that wonderful death, victory, triumph, and the looking forward to the glorious hope. And I want you, if it is possible at all, to get rid of your religion.

It has been so-called religion at all times that has slain and destroyed what was good. When Satan entered into Judas, the only people whom the devil could speak to through Judas were the priests, sad as it is to say. They conspired to get him to betray Jesus, and the devil took money from these priests to put Jesus to death. Now, it is a very serious thing, for we must clearly understand whether we are of the right spirit or not, for no man can be of the Spirit of Christ and persecute another; no man can have the true Spirit of Jesus and slay his brother, and no man can follow the Lord Jesus and have enmity in his heart. You cannot have Jesus and have bitterness and hatred, and persecute the believer.

It is possible for us, if we are not careful, to have within us an evil spirit of unbelief, and even in our best state it is possible for us to have enmity unless we are perfectly dead and we allow the life of the Lord to lead us. Remember how Jesus wanted to pass through a certain place as He was going to Jerusalem. Because He would not stop and preach to them concerning the kingdom, they refused to allow Him to go through their section of the country. And the disciples who were with Jesus said to Him, *"Lord, do You want us to command fire to come down from heaven and consume them, just as Elijah did?"* (Luke 9:54). But Jesus turned and said, *"You do not know what manner of spirit you are of"* (verse 55). There they were, following Jesus and with Him all the time, but Jesus rebuked that spirit in them.

I pray God that you will get this out of this service: that our knowledge of Jesus is pure love, and pure love for Jesus is death to self on all accounts—body, soul, and the human spirit. I believe that if we are in the will of God, we will be perfectly directed at all times, and if we desire to know anything about the mighty works of Christ, we will have to follow what Jesus said. Whatever He said came to pass.

KNOWING THE MIND OF GOD

Many things happened in the lives of the apostles to show His power over all flesh. In regard to paying taxes, Jesus said to Peter, "We are free, we can enter into the city without paying tribute;

nevertheless, we will pay." (See Matthew 17:24–27.) I like that thought, that Jesus was so righteous on all lines. It helps me a great deal. Then Jesus told Peter to do a very hard thing. He said, *"Take that hook and cast it into the sea. Draw out a fish, and take from its gills a piece of silver for you and Me"* (verse 27).

This was one of the hardest things Peter had to do. He had been fishing all his life, but never had he taken a coin out of a fish's mouth. There were thousands and millions of fish in the sea, but one fish had to have money in it. He went down to the sea as any natural man would, speculating and thinking, "How can it be?" But how could it not be, if Jesus said it would be? Then the perplexity would arise, "But there are so many fish! Which fish has the money?" Believer, if God speaks, it will be as He says. What you need is to know the mind of God and the Word of God, and you will be so free that you will never find a frown on your face or a tear in your eye.

The more you know of the mightiness of revelation, the more every fear will pass away. To know God is to be in the place of triumph. To know God is to be in the place of rest. To know God is to be in the place of victory. Undoubtedly, many things were in Peter's mind that day, but thank God there was one fish that had the silver piece, and Peter obeyed. Sometimes, to obey in blindness brings the victory. Sometimes, when perplexities arise in your mind, obedience means God working out the problem. Peter cast the hook into the sea, and it would have been amazing if you could have seen the disturbance the other fish made to move out of the way, all except the right one. God wanted just one among the millions of fish. God may put His hand upon you in the midst of millions of people, but if He speaks to you, the thing that He says will be appointed.

On this same occasion, Jesus said to Peter and the others that when they went out into the city they would see a man bearing a pitcher of water, and they should follow him. (See Mark 14:13.) In those days, it was not customary in the East for men to carry anything on their heads. The women always did the carrying, but this had to be a man, and he had to have a pitcher.

I know of one preacher who said that it was quite all right for Jesus to arrange for a colt to be tied before He ever instructed His disciples to go and find it. Another preacher said it was quite easy for Jesus to feed those thousands of people with the five loaves, because the loaves in those days were so tremendously big, but he didn't say that it was a little boy who had been carrying the five loaves. Unbelief can be very blind, but faith can see through a stone wall. Faith, when it is moved by the power of God, can laugh when trouble is near.

The disciples said to the man with the pitcher, *"Where is the guest room?"* (verse 14). "How strange it is that you should ask," the man must have replied. "I have been preparing that room, wondering who needed it." When God is leading, it is marvelous how perfectly everything works into the plan. He was arranging everything. You think He cannot do that today for you? For you who have been in perplexities for days and days, God knows how to deliver you out of trouble; He knows how to be with you in the dark hour. He can make all things work together for good to those who love Him. (See Romans 8:28.) He has a way of arranging His plan, and when God comes in, you always know it was a day in which you lived in Him.

Oh, to live in God! There is a vast difference between living in God and living in speculation and hope. There is something better than hope, something better than speculation. *"The people who know their God shall be strong, and carry out great exploits"* (Daniel 11:32), and God wants us to know Him.

THE APPOINTED HOUR

"When the hour had come, He sat down, and the twelve apostles with Him" (Luke 22:14). *"When the hour had come"*—that was the most wonderful hour. There never was an hour, never will be an hour like that hour. What hour was it? It was an hour when all of creation passed under the blood, when all that ever lived came under the glorious covering of the blood. It was an hour of destruction of demon power. It was an appointed hour of life coming out of death. It was an hour when all the world was coming into emancipation by the blood. It was an hour in the world's history when it emerged from dark chaos. It was a wonderful hour! Praise God for that hour! Was it a dark hour? It was a dark hour for Him, but a wonderful light dawned for us. It was tremendously dark for the Son of Man, but, praise God, He came through it.

There are some things in the Scriptures that move me greatly. I am glad that Paul was a human being. I am glad that Jesus became a man. I am glad that Daniel was human, and I am also glad that John was human. You ask, "Why?" Because I see that whatever God has done for other people, He can do for me. And I find that God has done such wonderful things for other people that I am always expecting that these things are possible for me. Think about this. It is a wonderful thought to me.

Jesus said in that trying hour—hear it for a moment—*"With fervent desire I have desired to eat this Passover with you before I suffer"* (Luke 22:15). Desire? What could be His desire? It was His desire because of the salvation of the world, His desire because of the dethronement of the powers of Satan, His desire because He knew

He was going to conquer everything and make every man free who ever lived. It was a great desire, but what lay between Him and its fulfillment? Gethsemane lay between that and the cross!

Some people say that Jesus died on the cross. It is perfectly true, but is that the only place? Jesus also died in Gethsemane. That was the tragic moment! That was the place where He paid the debt. It was in Gethsemane, and Gethsemane was between Him and the cross. He had a desire to eat this Passover, and He knew that Gethsemane was between Him and the cross.

I want you to think about Gethsemane. There, alone and with the tremendous weight and the awful effect of all sin and disease upon that body, He cried out, *"If it is possible, let this cup pass from Me"* (Matthew 26:39). He could only save men when He was man, but here, like a giant who has been refreshed and is coming out of a great chaos of darkness, He comes forth: *"For this cause I was born"* (John 18:37). It was His purpose to die for the world.

Oh, believer, will it ever pass through your lips or your mind for a moment that you will not have a desire to serve Christ like that? Can you, under any circumstances, stoop to take up your cross fully, to be in the place of ridicule, to surrender anything for the Man who said He desired to eat the Passover with His disciples, knowing what it meant? It can only come out of the depths of love we have for Him that we can say right now, "Lord Jesus, I will follow You."

SPIRITUAL REVELATION

Oh, brother or sister, there is something very wonderful in the decision in your heart! God knows the heart. You do not always have to be on the housetop and shout to indicate the condition of your heart. He knows your inward heart. You say, "I would be ashamed not to be willing to suffer for a Man who desired to suffer to save me." *"With fervent desire"* (Luke 22:15), He said.

I know what it is to have the kingdom of heaven within me. Jesus said that even the least in the kingdom of heaven is greater than John the Baptist (see Matthew 11:11), meaning those who are under the blood, those who have seen the Lord by faith, those who know that by redemption they are made sons of God. I say to you, Jesus will never taste again until we are there with Him. The kingdom will never be complete—it could not be—until we are all there at that great Supper of the Lamb where there will be millions and trillions of the redeemed, which no man can count. We will be there when that Supper is taking place. I like to think of that.

I hope you will take one step into definite lines with God and believe it. It is an act of faith that God wants to bring you into, a perfecting of that love that will always avail. It is a fact that He has opened the kingdom of heaven to all believers and that He gives eternal life to those who believe. The Lord, the omnipotent God, knows the end from the beginning and has arranged by the blood of the Lamb to cover the guilty and to make intercession for all believers. Oh, it is a wonderful inheritance of faith to find shelter under the blood of Jesus!

I want you to see that He says, *"Do this in remembrance of Me"* (Luke 22:19). He took the cup, He took the bread, and He gave thanks. The very attitude of giving thanks for His shed blood, giving thanks for His broken body, overwhelms the heart. To think that my Lord could give thanks for His own shed blood! To think that my Lord could give thanks for His own broken body! Only divinity can reveal this sublime act unto the heart!

The natural man cannot receive this revelation, but the spiritual man, the man who has been created anew by faith in Christ, is open to it. The man who believes that God comes in has the eternal seed of truth and righteousness and faith born into him. From the moment that he sees the truth on the lines of faith, he is made a new creation. The flesh ceases; the spiritual man begins. One is taken off, and the other is taken on, until a man is in the presence of God. I believe that the Lord brings a child of faith into a place of rest, causes him to sit with Him in heavenly places, gives him a language in the Spirit, and makes him know that he no longer belongs to the law of creation.

Do you see the bread that represents His broken body? The Lord knew He could not bring us any nearer to His broken body. The body of Jesus was made of that bread, and He knew He could bring us no nearer. He took the natural elements and said, "This bread represents my broken body." (See Luke 22:19.) Now, will it ever become that body of Christ? No, never. You cannot make it so. It is foolishness to believe it, but I receive it as an emblem. When I eat it, the natural leads me into the supernatural, and instantly I begin to feed on the supernatural by faith. One leads me into the other.

Jesus said, *"Take, eat; this is My body"* (Matthew 26:26). I have a real knowledge of Christ through this emblem. May we take from the table of the riches of His promises. The riches of heaven are before us. Fear not, only believe, for God has opened the treasures of His holy Word.

As the disciples were all gathered together with Jesus, He looked on them and said right into their ears, *"One of you will betray Me"* (verse 21). Jesus knew who would betray Him. He had known it for many, many months. They whispered to one another, "Who is it?" None of them had real confidence that it would not be he. That is the serious part about it; they had so little confidence in their ability to face the opposition that was before them, and they had no confidence that it would not be one of them.

Jesus knew. I can imagine that He had been talking to Judas many times, rebuking him and telling him that his course would surely bring him to a bad end. Jesus never had told any of His disciples, not even John who *"leaned on His breast"* (John 21:20). Now, if that same spirit of keeping things secret was in any church, it would purify the church. But I fear sometimes that Satan gets the advantage, and things are told before they are true. I believe God wants to so sanctify us, so separate us, that we will have that perfection of love that will not speak ill of a brother, that we will not slander a fellow believer whether it is true or not.

There was strife among them as to who should be the greatest, but He said, *"He who is greatest among you, let him be as the younger, and he who governs as he who serves"* (Luke 22:26). Then He, the Master, said, *"I am among you as the One who serves"* (verse 27). He, the noblest, the purest, was the servant of all! Exercising lordship over another is not of God. We must learn in our hearts that fellowship, true righteousness, loving one another, and preferring one another, must come into the church. Pentecost must outreach everything that ever has been, and we know it will if we are willing.

MOVING TOWARD PERFECTION

But it cannot be if we do not will it. We can never be filled with the Holy Spirit as long as there is any human craving for our own wills. Selfishness must be destroyed. Jesus was perfect, the end of everything, and God will bring us all there. It is giving that pays; it is helping that pays; it is loving that pays; it is putting yourself out for another person that pays.

> *I am among you as the One who serves. But you are those who have continued with Me in My trials. And I bestow upon you a kingdom, just as My Father bestowed one upon Me.*
>
> (Luke 22:27–29)

I believe there is a day coming that will be greater than anything any of us have any conception of. This is the testing road. This is the place where your whole body has to be covered with the wings of God so that your nakedness will not be seen. This is the thing that God is getting you ready for, the most wonderful thing your heart can imagine. How can you get into it? First of all, "*You…have continued with Me in My trials*" (verse 28). Jesus had been in trials; He had been in temptation. There is not one of us who is tempted beyond what He was. (See Hebrews 4:15.)

If a young man can be so pure that he cannot be tempted, he will never be fit to be made a judge, but God intends us to be so purified during these evil days that He can make us judges in the world to come. If you can be tried, if you can be tempted on any line, Jesus said, "*You are those who have continued with Me in My trials*" (Luke 22:28). Have faith, and God will keep you pure in the temptation.

How will we reach it? In Matthew 19:28, Jesus said,

> *In the regeneration, when the Son of Man sits on the throne of His glory, you who have followed Me will also sit on twelve thrones, judging the twelve tribes of Israel.*

Follow Him in constant regeneration. Every day is a regeneration; every day is a day of advancement; every day is a place of choice.

Every day you find yourself in need of fresh consecration. If you are in a place to yield, God moves you in the place of regeneration.

For years and years God has been making me appear to hundreds and thousands of people as a fool. I remember the day when He saved me and when He called me out. If there is a thing God wants to do today, He wants to be as real to you and me as He was to Abraham. After I was saved, I joined a church that consisted of a very lively group of people who were full of a revival spirit, and it was marvelous how God blessed us. And then there came a lukewarmness and indifference, and God said to me as clearly as anything, "Come out." I obeyed and came out. The people said, "We cannot understand you. We need you now, and you are leaving us."

The Plymouth Brethren at that time were in a conference. The Word of God was with them in power; the love of God was with them unveiled. Baptism by immersion was revealed to me, and when my friends saw me go into the water, they said I was altogether wrong. But God had called me, and I obeyed. The day came when I saw that the people of that church had dropped down to the letter of the law, only the letter, dry and barren.

At that time the Salvation Army was filled with love, filled with power, filled with zeal; every place was a revival, and I joined up with them. For about six years, the glory of God was there, and then the Lord said again, "Come out," and I was glad I came. It dropped right into a social movement, and God has no place for a social movement. We are saved by regeneration, and the man who is going on with God has no time for social reforms.

God moved on, and at that time there were many people who were receiving the baptism of the Holy Spirit without signs. Those days were days of heaven on earth. God unfolded the truth, showed the way of sanctification by the power of the blood of Christ, and in that I saw the great inflow of the life of God.

I thank God for that, but God came along again and said, "Come out." I obeyed God and went with what others called the "tongues folks"; they were regarded as having further light. I saw God orchestrating every movement I made, and even in this Pentecostal work, unless we see there is a real death, I can see that God will say to us, "Come out." Unless Pentecostalism wakes up to shake herself free from all worldly things and comes into a place of divine likeness with God, we will hear the voice of God saying, "Come out." He will have something far better than this.

I ask every one of you, Will you hear the voice of God and come out? You ask, "What do you mean?" Every one of you, without exception, knows that the only meaning of Pentecost is being on fire. If you are not on fire, you are not in the place of regeneration. It is only the fire of God that burns up the entanglements of the world.

When we came into this new work, God spoke to us by the Spirit, and we knew we had to reach the place of absolute yieldedness and cleansing, so that there would be nothing left. We were *"swept, and put in order"* (Matthew 12:44). Believer, that was only the beginning, and if you have not made tremendous progress in that holy zeal and power and compassion of God, we can truly say you have backslidden in heart. The backslider in heart is dead. He does not have the open vision. The backslider in heart does not see the Word of God in a fresher light every day. You can say that a man is a backslider in heart if he is not hated by the world. If you have the applause of the world, you do not have the approval of God.

A PLACE PREPARED FOR YOU

I do not know whether you will receive it or not, but my heart burns with the message of changing in the regeneration, for when you are changed, you will get a place in the kingdom to come where you will be in authority. This is the place that God has prepared for us, the place that is beyond all human conception. We can catch a glimpse of this glory when we see how John worshipped the angel, and the angel said to him, *"See that you do not do that! I am your fellow servant, and of your brethren who have the testimony of Jesus"* (Revelation 19:10). This angel was showing John the wonders of the glorious kingdom, and in the angel's glorified state, John thought the angel was the Lord. I wonder if we dare believe for it.

Let me close with these words: *"As we have borne the image of the man of dust, we shall also bear the image of the heavenly Man"* (1 Corinthians 15:49). To us, this means that everything of an earthly type has to cease, for the heavenly type is so wonderful in all its purity. God is full of love, full of purity, full of power. But there is no power in purity itself! There is no open door into heaven only on the basis of the void of sin between man and God. The heavens open only where the Spirit of the Lord is so leading that flesh has no power. But we will live in the Spirit. God bless you and prepare you for greater days.

30

The Riches of His Glory

ay the Lord of Hosts so surround us with revelation and blessing that our bodies get to the place where they can scarcely
contain the joys of the Lord. He will bring us to so rich a place of
divine order that forever we will know we are only the Lord's. What
a blessed state of grace to be brought into, where we know that the
body, the soul, the spirit are preserved blameless until the coming
of the Lord! Paul took us one step higher and said, *"May your whole
spirit, soul, and body be preserved blameless at the coming of our Lord"*
(1 Thessalonians 5:23). What a blessed state of grace!

When our hearts are moved to believe God, God is greatly desirous for us to have more of His presence. We have only one purpose
in mind in these meetings, and that is to strengthen you, to build
you up in the most holy faith, and to present you for every good
work so that you should be faultless in Him, quickened by the might
of the Spirit, so that you might be prepared for everything that God

279

has for you in the future. Our human nature may be brought to a place where it is so superabundantly attended to by God that in the body we will know nothing but the Lord of Hosts.

To this end, I bring you to the banquet that cannot be exhausted, a supply beyond all human thought, an abundance beyond all human extravagances. No matter how you come into great faith and believing in God, God says, "Much more abundantly, much more." So, I trust you will be moved to believe for more.

Are you ready? What for? That you might by the power of God be brought into His coffers with a new plan of righteousness, that you might be able as never before to leave the things of the world behind you and press on toward the prize of the high calling. (See Philippians 3:13–14).

Are you ready? What for? That you might be so in God's plan that you will feel God's hand upon you. You will know that He has chosen you, so that you might be a firstfruit unto God.

Are you ready? What for? That the Lord will have His choice, that His will and purpose will be yours, that the "Amen" of His character may sweep through your very nature, and that you may know as you have never known before that this is the day of the visitation between you and Him.

FROM HUMAN TO DIVINE

The Lord has been speaking to me about this meeting, and I believe we are going to study a Scripture that will be pleasing to Him, the third chapter of Ephesians.

I thank God for this stupendous, glorious exit of human into divine. I praise God for these studies, which are showing us the fullness of the pleasure of God.

It is the God of all grace who is bending over us with the fullness of recognition. He sees us; He knows us; He is acquainted with us. He is bending over us so that His infinite pleasure, His glorious, exhaustless pleasure may move us today. What can please Him more than to see His sons and daughters clothed, in their right mind (see Luke 8:35), listening to His voice, their eyes and ears awake, coming into the treasury of the Most High?

> *For this reason I, Paul, the prisoner of Christ Jesus for you Gentiles; if indeed you have heard of the dispensation of the grace of God which was given to me for you, how that by revelation He made known to me the mystery...which in other ages was not made known to the sons of men, as it has now been revealed by the Spirit to His holy apostles and prophets: that the Gentiles should be fellow heirs, of the same body, and partakers of His promise in Christ through the gospel. (Ephesians 3:1–3, 5–6)*

Oh, that we might be so clothed upon by the ministry of His grace, that we might so understand the mystery of His wonderful initiative! If only we could comprehend today more than ever before why the Gentiles have been brought into the glories of His treasury, to feed on the finest of the wheat, to drink at the riches of His pleasure, to be filled with the God of love that has no measure.

Without doubt, the greatest mystery of all time from the commencement of creation to now is Christ made manifest in human flesh. What can be greater than eternal life working mightily through eternal death? What can there be greater than the nature and appearance of Adam being changed by a new nature that has to be the fullness of the expression of the Father in heaven? *"And as we have borne the image of the man of dust, we shall also bear the image of the heavenly"* (1 Corinthians 15:49).

Everybody recognizes the Adamic race, but may God today let us understand fullness, the divine reflection. May He put us in the glorious position so that we may be changed—the living manifestation of the power of God changing our vestige. May He allow us to see the very expression of the Father, until the terrestrial will pass away, the celestial will come, and the rightness of His glory will press through all our humanity. Heaven will have an exhibition in us that it never before could have, and all the saints will be gathered. The very expression of the Master's face and the very glory of the Father will be in us.

INTERPRETATION OF TONGUES

It is the life from heaven that changes what could not be changed. Only the very expression of the nature of the God of all grace moving in our human faculties makes us know that we are begotten from above, changed by His power, transformed by His love, until we are not, for God has taken us. (See Genesis 5:24.)

Be still, for the grace that has come upon you is to so transform your fashion and so beautify your comeliness until right within you there will be the expression of the glory of God in the old creation, making the new creation just longing to depart.

Oh, that the breath of heaven would move us today until we would feel, whatever happened, that we must move on to get ready for exit!

OUR JOINT INHERITANCE

The fullness of the expression of the Holy Spirit order today is giving us a glimpse into what has been provided by the Father. We know that in the old Israel, from Abraham right down, God had a very special position. I am speaking now not of the mixed company but of those of whom Jesus said, "Is not this a daughter of Abraham?" (See Luke 13:16.) Paul spoke about it, knowing that he belonged to that royal aristocracy of Abraham's seed.

But the Gentiles had no right to it. The Master said to the Syrophenician woman, "Shall I take the bread of the children and give it to dogs?" (See Mark 7:27.) Did Jesus mean that the Gentiles were dogs? No, He did not mean that, but He meant that the whole race of the Gentiles knew that they were far below the standard and the order of those people who belonged to the royal stock of Israel. The Samaritans all felt it.

"But isn't it possible for the dogs to have some crumbs?" was the woman's question. (See verse 28.)

God has something better than crumbs. God has turned to the Gentiles, and He has made us of the same body, the same heirs. He has put no difference between them and us, but He has joined us up in that blessed order of coming into the promise through the blood of Christ.

Thank God! He met the need of all nations, of all ranks, of all conditions, and God so manifests His power that He has brought us into oneness, and we know we are sharing in the glory. We are sharing in the inner expression; we are sharing that beautiful position in which we know that we belong to the aristocracy of the church of God.

I want to bring you into very blessed privileges along these lines, for I want especially to deal with the knowledge of the inner working of that joint fellowship in this holy order with Christ. *"As it has now been revealed by the Spirit to His holy apostles and prophets"* (Ephesians 3:5).

I want you to see that this revelation was given by the power of the Spirit, and I want you to keep in mind that revelations are within the very body where Christ is manifested in the body. When Christ becomes the very personality of the fullness of the Father's will, then the Spirit, the effectual working of the power of God, has such glorious liberty in the body to unfold the mystery and the glories of the kingdom, for it is given to the Holy Spirit to reveal them as He reveals them all in Christ.

It is wonderful to know that I am in the body. It is wonderful to know that the apostles and prophets and all those who have passed down the years, holding aloft the torch, going on from victory to victory, all will be in the body. But how wonderful if we may be in the body so that we might be chosen out of the body to be the bride! It will be according as you are yielded to the *"effective working of His power"* (verse 7).

POWER THAT BRINGS LIGHT AND LIFE

"The effective working of His power" means to say that it is always Godward. The Holy Spirit has no alternative; He is here to fulfill the Great Commission of the Executive of heaven. Therefore, He is in the body for one express purpose: to make us understand the fullness of the glories that are contained in what is in us, which is Christ in us—not only the hope of glory (see Colossians 1:27), but also all the powers of the manifestation of the glory of Christ to be revealed in us.

It is for us to know the mysteries that have been laid up for us. It is for us to know the glories that will be revealed in Christ. It is for us to know all the fullness of the expression of His deity within us. It is for us to know that in this purposing of Christ's being in us, we have to be loosed from everything else, and He has to be manifesting and declaring to us. We have to be subservient, so that He may reign, rule, and have perfect authority, until in the body we are reigning over principalities and powers and every evil thing in the world.

The greatest mystery that has ever been known in the world, or ever will be known, is not only the spiritual body, but it is also the Gospel that has a creative power within it that brings light, liberty, immortality, and life. It is not only that, but it is also that after the seed, which is the life of the Son of God, has been put within you, Christ may be so formed in you that every revelation God has designed is for you because of His divine power in the body.

After the revelation came, after God began speaking to Paul, he felt so unworthy of this that he said, "[I] *am less than the least of all the saints*" (Ephesians 3:8). There is nothing but revelation that will take you to humility. If ever it goes the other way, it is because you have never yet under any circumstances been brought to a death like that of Christ.

All lifts, all summits, all glories, all revelation is in the death, when we are so dead to selfishness and self-desire, when we absolutely have been brought to the place of worthlessness and helplessness. Then, in that place, the power of the Holy Spirit works mightily through us.

"Less than the least of all the saints." What a blessed state of grace! Paul did not assert himself in any way. It did not matter where he

saw the saint, he said, "I am less worthy than that." Oh, what a sub-mission! How the principle of Christ was working through him!

Jesus knew that He was cooperating, perfectly united, that there was not a thing between Him and His Father, so He was in perfect order. Yet He *"made Himself of no reputation"* (Philippians 2:7). He submitted Himself to the Father, and just in the submission of going down, down, down, even to the death of the cross, God said to Him: "Oh, my Son! You are worthy of ten thousand thrones. You are worthy of all I have, and I will give you a name above every name."

There is not a name like the name of Jesus. All through eternity, that name will swing through the great anthems when they bring all the singers and all the angels, and there will be one song above all, *"To Him who loved us"* (Revelation 1:5).

May that make you the least of all saints, make you feel, "How can I submit myself to God so He can have royal preeminence, so that I will not refer to myself but He will be glorified?"

Isn't Jesus lovely? It pleased the Father to give Him the place. Nothing but humility will do it. Always be careful when you begin bouncing about, thinking you are somebody. More grace means more death to self; more life means more submission; more revelation means more baseness.

Why? That the excellency of the power, of the light, of the glory, may be exhibited. It is not I, but Another.

And thus it is proper for Christ to fulfill all righteousness in our human bodies, so that we may come to a place where we cease to be, for God's Son has to be royal; He has to be all and in all.

All in all! All in all!
Strength in time of weariness,
A light where shadows fall;
All in all! All in all!
Jesus is my all in all.

Christ wants to be glorified right in your mortal bodies, so that there will be a manifestation of this very revelation of Christ in you, the hope, the evidence of eternal glory.

A VISION OF THE CHURCH

For what purpose is the church formed together? That the Lord's people should be in the great mystery. Abraham, Isaac, Jacob, and the twelve patriarchs laid wonderful store upon the promise of God, and there was no hope for us Gentiles at all. But they missed the opportunity. They might have gone on to have been the greatest miracle workers, the most profound teachers of the truth. They might have been everywhere, all over the world, bringing such glorious revivals, because they were entrusted to it. But they failed God.

A very few of the apostles—when there was no open door for the Gospel, when their bodies were just filled with luminous light and the power of God pressing them right on—felt sure that that inward power was not meant to be exploded at nothing, so God moved upon them to turn to the Gentiles. Then a special revelation was given to Paul that God had joined up all the Gentiles.

My daughter often speaks of the ebony that will be around the throne because of the Africans who will be there. The Chinese will look very lovely around the throne, too, and the Japanese. All nations, peoples, kindred, and tongues are to be in the great body in heaven—all nationalities, all colors. What a blending of beauty in the glory, when all races will be filled with the glory, each and every one in its own nationality and yet in the express image of the Father! What a sight!

It is coming. It is already working in the body, and the body is feeling now that we are members in particular. In order that there will be no schism in the body, the Holy Spirit must have a royal place, effectively working through your mind, through your will, through every member of your body, until, as the Word of God says, every part of you is sanctified for the purpose that He may have preeminence. God will work in you, mightily through you, in all ways making manifestation in the human flesh—Christ in you!

YOUR PART IN THE BODY

You have the vision of the body; now I want you to get the vision of your personality in the body. There is no greater language than this about the Lord, that all fullness dwells in Him. (See Colossians 1:19.) Christ is to be a manifestation in humanity, with all fullness.

Do not be afraid of claiming your right. It is not a measure that you have come to. Remember, John saw Him, and he said that he had a measure that could not be measured. Christ is coming to us with this measure that cannot be measured. Human calculation will not do.

Paul went on to say this remarkable thing: that we may be able to have some revelation of the mightiness of God in its fullness.

To me, who am less than the least of all the saints, this grace was given, that I should preach among the Gentiles the unsearchable riches of Christ, and to make all see what is the fellowship of the mystery, which from the beginning of the ages has been hidden in God who created all things through Jesus Christ; to the intent.... (Ephesians 3:8–10)

God would have us to understand that those mighty words are to a certain intent. What is the intent?

To the intent that now the manifold wisdom of God might be made known by the church to the principalities and powers in the heavenly places. (verse 10)

The church is rising in all her vision and destroying the powers of darkness, ruling among the powers of wickedness, and transforming darkness to light by the power of the new creation in us. The church is doing all this to the intent that we might know the power that is working in us by the resurrection of the life of Christ.

So we are enriched with all enrichment; we are endued with all beatitudes; we are covered with all the graces; and now we are coming into all the mysteries, that the gifts of the Spirit may be so manifested in us that we might be a constancy of firstfruit.

People are always asking me what I belong to. It makes a lot of difference—they either have plenty of room for your company or not, it all depends where you belong. So I always say, and they do not seem to understand it, "I will give you my credentials, they are right here. I wrote them down so that I would always have them ready. They are, 'T.S.E.W.S.A.' "Oh! We never knew there were a people that had such credentials. What are they?"

"THE SECT EVERY WHERE SPOKEN AGAINST."

Glory to God! To the intent that this sect everywhere spoken against might be envisioned by an incarnation of glorious authority, Christ is in us mightier than death, mightier than sin, triumphing over principalities and powers.

There can be within you a mighty moving of this intent, of this habitual, divine activity of Christ being manifested in you, which was the revelation of Paul.

The second revelation of Paul, which never from the foundation of the world had been revealed, is that the Son of God, the very embodiment of the nature of the Most High, the very incarnation of His presence and power, could fill a human vessel to its utmost capacity, until the very nature of Him will sweep through by the power of God in the body.

You cannot enter into this without being enlarged, abounding, and superabundant. Everything in God is enlargement. God never wants a child of His in the world to be measured. You cannot measure your place. You might measure your land, you might measure your harvest, but you cannot measure the purposes of the Spirit life: they are boundless; they are infinite. They are for the finite, but all the riches of God are infinite and boundless. There is no such thing as measuring them. If ever you measure God, you will be thin and little and dwarfed. You cannot measure. You have an exhaustless place.

God's Son is in you with all the power of development, until you are so enriched by this divine grace that you live in the world knowing that God is transforming you from grace to grace, from victory to victory.

The Spirit in you has no other foundation than from glory unto glory. Paul was so enlarged in the Spirit in this third chapter of Ephesians that his language failed to go on. And then, when he failed to go on in his language, he bowed his knees unto the Father. Oh, this is supreme! This is beyond all that could be! When language failed, when prophecy had no more room, it seems that he came to a place where he got down on his knees. Then we hear by the power of the Spirit language beyond all Paul could ever say: *"For this reason I bow my knees to the Father of our Lord Jesus Christ, from whom the whole family in heaven and earth is named"* (Ephesians 3:14–15).

Paul realized that he was joining earth and heaven together. They are one, thank God! There is nothing between us and heaven. Gravity may hold us, but all in heaven and in earth are joined under one blood, with no division or separation. *"To be absent from the body* [is] *to be present with the Lord"* (2 Corinthians 5:8).

MORE THAN WHAT YOU EXPECT

God has something here for us in the language of the Holy Spirit. He wants it to enlarge our hearts and take a breath of heaven. Let your whole soul reach out unto God; dare to breathe in heaven; dare to be awakened to all God's mind; listen to the language of the Holy Spirit. Paul was praying in the Spirit:

That He would grant you, according to the riches of His glory, to be strengthened with might through His Spirit in the inner man, that Christ may dwell in your hearts through faith; that you, being rooted and grounded in love, may be able to comprehend with all the saints what is the width and length and depth and height; to know the love of Christ which passes knowledge; that you may be filled with all the fullness of God. Now to Him who is able to do exceedingly abundantly above all that we ask or think, according to the power that works in us, to Him be glory in the church by Christ Jesus to all generations, forever and ever. Amen. (Ephesians 3:16–21)

This is the Gentile's inhabitation; this is the Gentile's position; this is the body that is being joined up—this spiritual body that has to come into a fullness beyond all expectations.

You cannot expect the fullness that He has waiting for you. If you cannot think of it, then I am sure you cannot expect it. If you cannot ask, then I am sure it is larger than you can expect.

The Holy Spirit takes these things and brings them before us this morning, to the intent that this wonderful, divine appointment will be ours.

How may I get nearer to God? How may I be in the place of helplessness—in my own place and dependent on God? I see a tide rising. *"Blessed are the poor in spirit, for theirs is the kingdom of heaven"* (Matthew 5:3). God is making us very poor, but we are rich in it because our hands are stretched out toward Him in this holy day of His visitation to our hearts.

Believe that He is in you. Believe that He is almightiness. Believe that He is all fullness. Then let yourself go until He is on the throne of your heart. Let everything submit itself to God's throne and the King. Yield yourself unto Him in so sublime a position that He is in perfect order over everything. Let God have His perfect way through you. If you will let go, God will take hold and keep you up.

Oh, to seek only the will of God, to be only in the purpose of God, to seek only that God will be glorified, and not I! We need to repeat the words over and over in our hearts: "Not I, but Christ." (See Galatians 2:20.)

How did it come to Paul? It came when he was *"less than the least of all the saints"* (Ephesians 3:8). The effective working of the power when he was *"less than the least of all the saints"* buoyed him up until God was manifested in that mortal flesh, for surely Paul reached into all the fullness of that mighty God.

I believe God wants to send you away filled with the Spirit. Oh, beloved, are you ready? What must you do? You must say, "Father, have your way. Do not let my human will spoil your divine plan. Father, take charge of me today in such a way that I will be wholly, entirely on the altar for Your service." And I am sure He will meet you in this.

About the Author

A n encounter with Smith Wigglesworth (1859–1947) was an un-
forgettable experience. This seems to be the universal reaction
of all who knew him or heard him speak. Smith Wigglesworth was
a simple yet remarkable man who was used in an extraordinary way
by our extraordinary God. He had a contagious and inspiring faith.
Under his ministry, thousands of people came to salvation, committed themselves to a deeper faith in Christ, received the baptism
in the Holy Spirit, and were miraculously healed. The power that
brought these kinds of results was the presence of the Holy Spirit, who filled Smith Wigglesworth and used him in bringing the
good news of the Gospel to people all over the world. Wigglesworth
gave glory to God for everything that was accomplished through his
ministry, and he wanted people to understand his work only in this
context, because his sole desire was that people would see Jesus and
not himself.

Smith Wigglesworth was born in England in 1859. Immediately after his conversion as a boy, he had a concern for the salvation of others and won people to Christ, including his mother. Even so, as a young man, he could not express himself well enough to give a testimony in church, much less preach a sermon. Wigglesworth said that his mother had the same difficulty in expressing herself that he did. This family trait, coupled with the fact that he had no formal education because he began working twelve hours a day at the age of seven to help support the family, contributed to Wigglesworth's awkward speaking style. He became a plumber by trade, yet he continued to devote himself to winning many people to Christ on an individual basis.

In 1882, he married Polly Featherstone, a vivacious young woman who loved God and had a gift of preaching and evangelism. It was she who taught him to read and who became his closest confidant and strongest supporter. They both had compassion for the poor and needy in their community, and they opened a mission, at which Polly preached. Significantly, people were miraculously healed when Wigglesworth prayed for them.

In 1907, Wigglesworth's circumstances changed dramatically when, at the age of forty-eight, he was baptized in the Holy Spirit. Suddenly, he had a new power that enabled him to preach, and even his wife was amazed at the transformation. This was the beginning of what became a worldwide evangelistic and healing ministry that reached thousands. He eventually ministered in the United States, Australia, South Africa, and all over Europe. His ministry extended up to the time of his death in 1947.

Several emphases in Smith Wigglesworth's life and ministry characterize him: a genuine, deep compassion for the unsaved and sick; an unflinching belief in the Word of God; a desire that Christ should increase and he should decrease (John 3:30); a belief that he was called to exhort people to enlarge their faith and trust in God; an emphasis on the baptism in the Holy Spirit with the manifestation of the gifts of the Spirit as in the early church; and a belief in complete healing for everyone of all sickness.

Smith Wigglesworth was called "The Apostle of Faith" because absolute trust in God was a constant theme of both his life and his messages. In his meetings, he would quote passages from the Word of God and lead lively singing to help build people's faith and encourage them to act on it. He emphasized belief in the fact that God could do the impossible. He had great faith in what God could do, and God did great things through him.

Wigglesworth's unorthodox methods were often questioned. As a person, Wigglesworth was reportedly courteous, kind, and gentle. However, he became forceful when dealing with the devil, whom he believed caused all sickness. Wigglesworth said the reason he spoke bluntly and acted forcefully with people was that he knew he needed to get their attention so they could focus on God. He also had such anger toward the devil and sickness that he acted in a seemingly rough way. When he prayed for people to be healed, he would often hit or punch them at the place of their problem or illness. Yet, no one was hurt by this startling treatment. Instead, they were remarkably healed. When he was asked why he treated people in this manner, he said that he was not hitting the people but that he was hitting the devil. He believed that Satan should never be treated gently or allowed to get away with anything. About twenty people were reportedly raised from the dead after he prayed for them. Wigglesworth himself was healed of appendicitis and kidney stones, after which his personality softened and he was gentler with those who came to him for prayer for healing. His abrupt manner in ministering may be attributed to the fact that he was very serious about his calling and got down to business quickly.

Although Wigglesworth believed in complete healing, he encountered illnesses and deaths that were difficult to understand. These included the deaths of his wife and son, his daughter's lifelong deafness, and his own battles with kidney stones and sciatica.

He often seemed paradoxical: compassionate but forceful, blunt but gentle, a well-dressed gentleman whose speech was often ungrammatical or confusing. However, he loved God with everything he had, he was steadfastly committed to God and to His Word, and he didn't rest until he saw God move in the lives of those who needed Him.

In 1936, Smith Wigglesworth prophesied about what we now know as the charismatic movement. He accurately predicted that the established mainline denominations would experience revival and the gifts of the Spirit in a way that would surpass even the Pentecostal movement. Wigglesworth did not live to see the renewal, but as an evangelist and prophet with a remarkable healing ministry, he had a tremendous influence on both the Pentecostal and charismatic movements, and his example and influence on believers are felt to this day.

Without the power of God that was so obviously present in his life and ministry, we might not be reading transcripts of his sermons, for his spoken messages were often disjointed and ungrammatical. However, true gems of spiritual insight shine through them because of the revelation he received through the Holy Spirit. It was his life of complete devotion and belief in God and his reliance on the Holy Spirit that brought the life-changing power of God into his messages.

As you read this book, it is important to remember that Wigglesworth's works span a period of several decades, from the early 1900s to the 1940s. They were originally presented as spoken rather than written messages, and necessarily retain some of the flavor of a church service or prayer meeting. Some of the messages were Bible studies that Wigglesworth led at various conferences. At his meetings, he would often speak in tongues and give the interpretation, and these messages have been included as well. Because of Wigglesworth's unique style, the sermons and Bible studies in this book have been edited for clarity, and archaic expressions that would be unfamiliar to modern readers have been updated.

In conclusion, we hope that as you read these words of Smith Wigglesworth, you will truly sense his complete trust and unwavering faith in God and take to heart one of his favorite sayings: "Only believe!"

Welcome to Our House!

We Have a Special Gift for You ...

It is our privilege and pleasure to share in your love of Christian classics by publishing books that enrich your life and encourage your faith.

To show our appreciation, we invite you to sign up to receive a specially selected **Reader Appreciation Gift**, with our compliments. Just go to the Web address at the bottom of this page.

God bless you as you seek a deeper walk with Him!

WE HAVE A GIFT FOR YOU

whpub.me/classicthx

WHITAKER
HOUSE